ILLINOIS CENTRAL COLLEGE
PN1077.S35 1966
STACKS
Literature and occult tradition.

A12900 246832

W9-BCF-795

A12900 246832

PN
1077          SAURAT                    37222
.S35          Literature and occult
1966          tradition

PN
1077          SAURAT                    37222
.S35          Literature and occult
1966          tradition

MAY 3  76                    478401025
APR 6  77
          APR 6  77
LAS       SEP 1978  HOLOHAN  340-50-2335
          MAY 11 81          I F    363
                             I  22074

# WITHDRAWN

## Illinois Central College
## Learning Resource Center

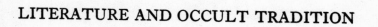
LITERATURE AND OCCULT TRADITION

# LITERATURE
# AND OCCULT TRADITION
## Studies in Philosophical Poetry

By

# DENIS SAURAT, 1890 - 1958

Professor of French Literature
in the University of London
King's College

Translated from the French
by
DOROTHY BOLTON

KENNIKAT PRESS, INC./PORT WASHINGTON, N. Y.

ILLINOIS CENTRAL COLLEGE
LEARNING RESOURCE CENTER

37222

PN
1077
.S35
1966

LITERATURE AND OCCULT TRADITION

Published in 1930
Reissued in 1966 by Kennikat Press

Library of Congress Catalog Card No: 65-27133

# CONTENTS

# CONTENTS

# I

# INTRODUCTION

## GENERAL PURPOSE OF THIS STUDY

PHILOSOPHICAL poetry is as ancient and as legitimate as philosophy itself. As soon as men began to think methodically, they realised that logical reason did not suffice to explain the universe and they invoked the aid of other faculties: imagination, intuition, poetry. These faculties existed, doubtless, long before philosophical poetry, but we cannot speak of philosophical poetry before they are allied to reason, properly so-called, when the intuitions of primitive myths have become clearer and have taken on a systematic and rational meaning in the human brain. It is the alliance of reason, intuition and myth which is the very foundation of philosophical poetry; a close and indissoluble alliance which gives to this human effort its unity, its force and its scope.

I propose, in this work, to study modern philosophical poetry. It was unquestionably a new intellectual race which made its appearance at the Renaissance, a race which, after the long training of the Middle Ages, came forth fully armed to conquer the world; and it did conquer it, at least

I

for a time. It is the philosophical poetry of this race which best expresses its most deeply rooted and powerful characteristic: its conception of the world and of life, that by which it is distinguished from all other races, the mental and spiritual attitude which enabled it to conquer the world and develop a material, scientific civilisation hitherto unprecedented. The representatives or champions of other races, often older in culture, sometimes more refined, perhaps more intelligent—who knows?—profess to despise this material and scientific civilisation, accuse it of having no soul. We shall see, on the contrary, that its soul is as noble as the human soul has ever been, and that it has expressed itself in strains as sublime and as deep as those of India herself; and we shall see, moreover, that from this very soul, from its attitude towards life, arose that scientific civilisation the possession of which has secured for our race the mastery of the world.

And it is certainly in the philosophical poetry of a race that its very soul can be seen. All other forms of art or science which have a practical aim are forced to specialise too much to be capable of representing more than a faculty or a point of view. Philosophy by itself is too critical, too analytical, too methodical; it is obliged to neglect aspirations for tangible results. Poetry by itself is too irresponsible and sentimental; its concern is too purely emotional just as that of philosophy is too purely critical. Each of the various sciences pursues its own special end; history, whether general or literary, is little more than retrospection.

Only in philosophical poetry does the soul of the race express itself synthetically, its dreams and its intelligence, its knowledge and its desires, before their necessary subdivision, impelling each intellectual need towards its own particular methods, obscures the first and ever fundamental unity. So, from time to time, there arises some superior genius, who, from the summit of the assembled results of the specialised branches of knowledge, obtains a vision of the far-off goals, expresses anew for his own time the desires of his fellow men, marks out the distance already covered or tries to divine the future ways. Thus Milton in the seventeenth century, Goethe in the eighteenth, Victor Hugo, Nietzsche and Whitman in the nineteenth. And only in philosophical poetry is it possible both to give utterance to aspirations and to record desires already expressed and results already achieved. For we are not dealing here with those great retrospections which the workers in each order make from time to time in order to see where they are; nor with a complete synthesis of all those great syntheses, a task requiring an erudition to which the human mind could not attain, or to which it could only attain, in any case, by giving up the right to the first and final vision. The philosophical poets are not scholars, they are not even

3

philosophers. Their synthesis is that of the desires. Appraising the results already achieved, regarding them as a whole in so far as they have influenced their age, often unaware of details, they see and express the contentment or the unsatisfied longings of the men of their own time. From far above and far away they mark out the suitable ways, preserving within themselves the simplicity as well as the strength and loftiness of the fundamental desires of the race. In spite of the gaps in their information, the defects in their intelligence, they have a right to our respect, we ought to give them a hearing. These gaps and defects, after all, vary in each one; and Milton and Goethe were fairly perfect types of human intelligence. Therefore, the philosophical poets remain, more than any other order of minds, best qualified to represent the entire aspirations of their race, the very soul of their humanity.

At the risk of being accused of having preconceived ideas, I prefer to indicate clearly at the beginning the conclusions arrived at in this work, to point out what, to my mind, constitutes the essential unity of all the facts we are going to study, what distinguishes modern philosophical poetry, that is to say in Europe and America from the Renaissance to our own day, from similar forms of art in classical times or in Asia:

Modern philosophical poetry is the expression, varying according to the character, intelligence

and surroundings of each poet, of a body of common ideas, related to neo-platonism and various
occult doctrines, but original in its essence which
represents the mind of modern man: the assertion
of the liberty of man and of the sanctity of material
nature of which he is a part.*

*In this volume is stated only the general theory on this
subject, and a first example is given in Spenser. My other
works on *Milton, Man and Thinker, Blake and Modern Thought*,
and *La Religion de Victor Hugo*, contain the detailed studies
which go to support the theory.

# II

# PHILOSOPHICAL POETRY

## I. BASIC IDEAS

### NON-CHRISTIAN RELIGIOUS ELEMENTS IN MODERN POETRY

#### I

ONE of the most curious phenomena of modern literature from the Renaissance to the nineteenth century is the existence among a certain number of great poets, between whom there is often but a slight direct connection, of a common, *non-Christian* stock of myths and of ideas. Spenser, Milton, Blake, Shelley, Emerson and Whitman in Anglo-Saxon literature; Goethe, Heine, Wagner, Nietzsche in Germany; Hugo, Vigny, Lamartine and Leconte de Lisle in France, would seem, after a close study of their religious ideas, in spite of an infinite divergence in detail, to be like branches of the same tree. The same general ideas are developed in their works, culminating at times in expressions which, though very far removed from each other, yet remain akin. Still more curious than the existence of ideas in common is the recurrence of certain myths and symbols

6

which seem to have a particular fascination for these poets.

Only a patient study of detail, disclosing both the variations and the resemblances, can prove this general assertion. In this broad survey I am obliged to allow myself a certain licence in the use of definitions, more or less taken for granted, of certain words and ideas: as ethnographers usually do when studying similar but not identical phenomena in different countries. I purposely allude to ethnography, for it is in part the aim of this study to establish the existence among such ultra-civilised beings as modern poets generally are, of ways of thinking often comparable to those of the "primitives."

From our point of view, one of the characteristics of poetry is lack of intellectual responsibility. A poet may be in earnest and believe firmly in what he says; he may also look upon his visions and ideas purely as artistic diversions, whether they are destined to serve as symbols or not. I will leave on one side, then, the question of actual belief: certain ideas, certain myths have, at any rate, aroused the interest of poets, whether they have taken them seriously (as is however often the case) or not. I am concerned here with the conceptions in themselves, with their propagation and their development rather than with the individual mind of the authors who adopted them or at times created them anew.

7

Moreover, I will proceed by considering groups of ideas rather than separate ideas. A certain idea in a certain author, taken individually, may not prove anything, or may come from a definite source and be of little interest. But if the author's ideas are examined as a whole, it is possible to see the tendencies at work in his mind. A certain trait which might be only a distortion of a Christian idea appears then in its proper light to be more closely connected with a wider current outside the Christian tradition. With the exception of Spenser and Lamartine (and even in them the most curious religious elements are not orthodox), the poets named above are not Christian in thought. One might include the conceptions of Milton and Emerson among the Christian heresies; but to do so would be to limit their horizon considerably. Milton by his connection with the Cabala, Emerson by seeking his inspiration in India, definitely departed from Christianity.

Let us try to see the general features of the doctrine more or less held in common by all these poets. If, as I have asked that it should be, the meaning of words is stretched a little, they are all pantheists, starting out generally from the same conception of an inaccessible god with no perceptible relations with the world, acknowledging a demiurge or secondary deity whose business it is to look after the world and who is himself the entirety of the world. In almost all we find traces of the myth of the divine hermaphrodite in connection with this god, or of that of the incest which is often the consequence of it. Their pantheism has as a result the doctrine of the division of God into innumerable creatures, which generally renders all creatures equally divine and mortal or immortal in the same way, the feeling of kinship with animals being particularly striking. Various theories of reincarnation or return to earth after death play an important part in almost all. Nearly all are at one in acknowledging, as a consequence of these ideas, that matter and earthly life are good and satisfying, and they tend to suppress individual immortality in another world. The usual counterpart of the doctrine of the division of God, the reconstitution of divine unity by election, evolution or special creation of certain superior individuals conscious of some divine element within them is generally found. Finally, what is most striking of all, perhaps, is the community of moral ideas; nearly all are in revolt against the orthodox conception of God or against the moral law (or, at least, they have freely employed the poetic theme of rebellion, celebrating the fall or the death of the gods), and have preached liberty, justified sensuality and claimed for the individual the right to follow his inclinations, because these inclinations are divine.

Let us briefly examine, one by one, these general

9

conceptions. Spenser, when he speaks openly of God, tries to remain within the bounds of orthodoxy; his personal conceptions are to be found in the myths which he creates or adapts as he thinks fit. Writing in the sixteenth century, before it is possible to speak with any real accuracy of the formation of a modern mind, he is often to us merely a rudimentary starting point. We shall, later on, come across his conception of Nature. Let us note, in the first place, the curious fact that he attributes to Nature this quality of noumenon, intangible and unfathomable, which is generally reserved for the deity, as is the reconciliation of opposites. Probably, in speaking of this inoffensive entity "Nature," he feels more at liberty to express his ideas on the deity:

"This great grandmother of all creatures bred,
Great Nature, ever young, yet full of eld;
Still moving, yet unmoved from her sted;
Unseene of any, yet of all beheld."*

Nature is superior to Jupiter, the chief of the gods, and it is she who, being at the same time visible and invisible, gives final judgment when the Titaness *Change* aspires to universal empire. This universal empire does not belong to Nature herself: she is remote from the world, and when she disappears, no one can find her.

* *Faërie Queene*, Mutability Cantos, vii. 13.

"Then was that whole assembly quite dismist,
  And Natur's selfe did vanish, whither no man
  wist."*

In one of the last links of the poetic chain we again meet a very similar myth in Wagner's Erda, who in the *Ring* appears only once to give warning and once to judge:

> "Aus heimischer Tiefe
> Aus sinnendem Schlafe,"

and who says:

> "Mein Schlaf ist Träumen
> Mein Träumen Sinnen."

She manifested herself only in giving birth to Brunnhilde. She also is the embodiment of Nature as a whole.

> "Wo Wesen sind
> Weht dein Athem."

Only the power of the supreme god, Wotan, can make her appear, and, her judgment given, she too disappears into the abyss.

> "Whither, no man wist."

Milton's God is inaccessible, and is not manifest.†

---

* *Ibid.* vii. 59. Cf. Edwin Greenlaw in *Studies in Philology*, July 1920, pp. 320-359 (the University of North Carolina).

† In connection with Milton I have collected the appropriate passages in *Milton, Man and Thinker* (Cape, Dial Press),

"Fountain of Light, thyself invisible."
"But God, as he cannot be seen, so neither can he
be heard."

God does not create; the Creator is the Son: God
has no other attribute left but that of being, and
of being the incomprehensible source of everything.

Blake carries this idea still further. In the enormous mythology which he collected rather than
created he hardly speaks of God; he delegates
all his functions to secondary powers whom he
calls "The Eternals."

Shelley, whose entire work is permeated with
religious spirit, wrote a pamphlet on the *Necessity of Atheism*, and to the very end refused to acknowledge a personal God.*

The entire poem "Dieu," by Victor Hugo,† is
devoted to pointing out the inaccessibility of the
Supreme Being.

The God of the prologue of *Faust* is evidently
only a literary personage, and when Faust desires
to obtain from the Supreme Powers the return of
Helen, it is not to God but to the "Mothers" that
Mephistopheles sends him.

and in connection with Blake in *Blake and Modern Thought*
(Constable, Dial Press). See especially as regards Blake the
thesis of M. Berger, *William Blake, poésie et mysti cisme* (Paris
1907), p. 109 and *passim*.

  * Cf. Koszul, *La Jeunesse de Shelley*, pp. 121, 303-307.

  † See on Hugo, Saurat, *La Religion de Victor Hugo* (Hachette).

But the poets could hardly be content with this intangible God. The rejection of the idea of God in favour of the idea of noumenon led, in minds generally craving for definite symbols, to the rejection of the very idea of God, or to the degeneration of God into a personage of the order of Wagner's Erda.

For God was substituted (consciously and systematically this time, no longer after the manner of Spenser) Nature, Life or another similar entity, but without, however, any loss of religious feeling.

Thus Nietzsche, after Jean Paul, took up once more the deep yet amusing myth of the death of God.

Zarathustra, coming down from the mountain, mocks at the hermit, who is not yet aware that God is dead:*

"Dieser alte Heilige hat in seinem Walde noch nichts davon gehört, dass Gott tot ist."

And the old out-of-work pope, "ausser Dienst," explains to us, or at least gives Zarathustra the opportunity of explaining, "dass ihn das Mitleiden erwürgte, dass die Liebe zum Menschen seine Hölle und zuletzt sein Tod wurde."

But with an altogether mystic enthusiasm Nietzsche sings the praises of Life:

"In dein Auge schaute ich jüngst, O Leben!

* Also sprach Zarathustra, Vorrede 2, ausser Dienst, Nacht Lied.

Und ins Unergründliche schien ich mir da zu sinken."

As to Whitman, who also religiously extols Nature and Life, he sees beyond these:

"Santa Spirita, breather, life,
Beyond the light, lighter than light . . .
Including all life on earth—touching, includ-
ing God—including Saviour and Satan:
Ethereal, pervading all . . .
Essence of forms—life of the real identities,
permanent, positive (namely the unseen)."*

But he calmly declares:

"And I say to mankind: Be not curious about
God,
For I who am curious about each man am not
curious about God;"

because, first of all, it is impossible to know God, and then, because the poet sees God in all life:

"I hear and behold God in every object, yet
understand God not in the least."†

We find here the result of an evolution of ideas, whose beginning we witnessed when the poets seized hold of the conception of an inaccessible God.

Logically and historically, to the doctrines of

* " The Square Deific."
† " Song of Myself," 48.

14

the noumenon God is allied the theory of intermediary powers between God and creation. Some
of our poets pass straight from God to Nature;
but most of them conceive the existence of a sort
of Demiurge, an inferior creative and organising
God; and several even place intermediary powers
between the noumenon God and the active God.

Thus Erda in Wagner replies first of all to the
questions of Wotan:

"Mein Schlaf ist Träumen,
 Doch wenn ich schlafe,
 Wachen Nornen:
 Sie weben das Seil,
 Und spinnen fromm was ich weiss;
 Was fragst du nicht die Nornen?"

The Norns, as Wotan says in reply, do nothing
but carry out decrees, the causes of which are
higher than they are—in the Unfathomable.

In Goethe we find similar powers: the Mothers
(2nd *Faust*, *ll.* 1600 to 1680), who are, no doubt,
nearer to the noumenon:

"Um sie kein Ort, noch weniger eine Zeit;
 Von ihnen sprechen ist Verlegenheit.
 Die Mütter sind es."

However, one can approach them and obtain from
them what one desires: they bring back Helen
to life for Faust.

In Shelley, it is Demogorgon, an unknown and

terrible power, who is above Jupiter and who, when the time comes, overthrows "the Tyrant of the world."

Already to Milton Demogorgon was only a dreaded name; in "Prometheus Unbound," he is veiled on his throne of ebony, shapeless:

> "Ungazed upon and shapeless; neither limb, nor form, nor outline" (ii., iv. 5.)

He knows the real God who is not manifest but who is, however, to be found in Nature and in beings, and he knows that the God of the present world, Jupiter, will fall. He is the Minister of the Absolute. He replies to Jupiter, who asks him who he is:

> "Eternity. Demand no direr name."

In Blake, these intermediate powers are called the Eternals, whose names we hardly know; the one among them who has fallen has become the Demiurge, Urizen.* (Or, in an alternative scheme, Albion.)

The conception of this Demiurge, God of the world, Soul of the world, who may be called Earth, Nature, Life, etc., is a commonplace of philosophical poetry. We will not linger over it here; to do so to any purpose we should have to study in detail the ideas of each poet, and our object here

* Cp. Berger, p. 146 and following, and Saurat, *Blake and Modern Thought*.

is to seek more distinct traces of definite beliefs. Let us note, however, that this pantheism exists to a certain extent in almost all of them: to Milton the Demiurge is known as the Son; to Shelley as the Soul of the world; to Blake it is sometimes universal Man, sometimes Urizen; in Spenser, Goethe, Wagner, Nietzsche, Whitman, Hugo we have rather the feeling of it than the idea, or else the application of the idea in the poetry of Nature rather than the abstract idea. Without, therefore, allowing ourselves to be drawn into a discussion of the particular philosophy of each one, let us pick out the fragments of the ancient myths which remain common to all.

The most interesting point here is the survival in poetry of what the Cabalists call the "sexual law."*

The Demiurge creates the world or becomes the world by an act which, more or less vaguely, according to the poet considered, is a cosmic parallel to the sexual act. In its extreme expression we find the hermaphrodite God, who divides himself and whose parts fecundate each other; hence the theme of divine incest. Sometimes the feminine divinity is called the daughter and is fecundated by her father, sometimes it is the brother who fecundates the sister; sometimes the poet places the myth on the human plane while

* See Karppe, *Etude sur les origines et la nature du Zohar*, pp. 424-434.

keeping the incest; sometimes he keeps the sexual union without emphasising the incestuous feature. And, at bottom, all these cases and this sexual law itself are only special aspects of a wider theme to which we will return: the theme of the division of God, followed by the reconstitution of God.

Blake, as is often the case, is the one who gives us the myth in its most characterised form.

The Demiurges (there are several for Blake) begin by dividing themselves, amid unspeakable tortures, each one into male and female:

> "At length in tears and cries embodied
> A female born, trembling and pale
> All eternity shuddered at the sight
> Of the first Female now separate."

For Blake retained a curious feeling of primitive horror when visualising these conceptions, a horror intensified by the second act of the drama, the fecundation:

> "Eternity shuddered when they saw
> Man begetting his likeness
> On his own divided image."

"Man" being another name of the Demiurge. No other poet goes as far as that; but the various degrees of degradation of the myth are easily seen.

First of all, in Goethe, the name "Die Mütter" is curious; Goethe lays stress on it, and very artistically produces the feeling of a mystery which he does not wish to reveal. Faust is astonished at this name:

"Die Mütter! Mütter!—'s klingt so wunderlich!"

Are not the Mothers those same primitive deities fecundated at the beginning of the worlds by the Demiurges, whose issue they are? Goethe's thought is difficult to follow since he purposely veils it. But the expression of it belongs, in any case, to the myth we are tracking.

Spenser and Milton, when speaking of God, are naturally more reserved. Both of them, however, admit the presence, by the side of God, of a feminine power, his daughter, and they make sufficiently definite allusions to the rôle of this power. Spenser's Hymne IV introduces us to "Sapience":

"There in his bosome Sapience doth sit,
  The soveraine dearling of the Deity,
  And in her hand a scepter she doth hold,
  With which she rules the house of God on hy."

And the world is her issue:

"Both heaven and earth obey unto her will,
  And all the creatures which they both containe;
  For of her fulness, which the world doth fill,
  They all partook—
  Through observation of her high behest,
  By which they first were made and still in-
    creast."

19

Mr. Charles C. Osgood,* after a detailed study of this "Sapience," tries to trace back this personage to the platonist allegories or to the Bible, but not with entire success. We shall see that the rôle of Shekhina in the Cabala would explain the features of "Sapience" which remain doubtful. Milton, under the probable influence of both Spenser and the Cabala,† has a conception of the deity similar to theirs. He makes this clear in quite a long page of prose, in which he justifies man's need of woman by the reason that

"God himself conceals not his own recreations before the world was built: I was, said the Eternal Wisdom, daily his delight, playing always before him."‡

Sexual life exists within the deity himself. It exists also among the angels.§ And if Spenser and Milton are on their guard against making too definite assertions, which would seem disrespectful to the deity, they are not embarrassed by this consideration when dealing with lower powers. Milton gives us the myth in full detail in the allegory of Sin and Death in Book II of *Paradise Lost*. Satan has a daughter, Sin, springing directly

* *Studies in Philology* (University of North Carolina), April 1917, pp. 167-177.

† Cf. Saurat, *Milton et le matérialisme chrétien:* on Milton and the Zohar.

‡ Milton, *Prose*, Bohn, vol. iii. pp. 329-330.

§ *Paradise Lost*, iv. 750, etc. Very clear on this point.

from himself, as Minerva sprang from the brain of Jupiter. This daughter is fecundated by him and gives birth to Death. No sooner is Death born than he sets off in pursuit of his mother, who flees in horror, and he in his turn becomes the father of other monsters. We shall meet again, presently, this theme of pursuit.

Spenser develops this conception of divine sexual life in his myth of the garden of Adonis.* Venus's lover is kept hidden by her in a secret garden, which is the source of all life and all creatures spring from their union, for Venus is matter and Adonis is form, but things certainly take place on the sexual plane in what is one of the most magnificent cantos of the *Faërie Queene*. Note that here the "incest" theme has vanished.

Wagner gives us the myth in what is perhaps a still more primitive form. The incest which is the subject of the *Walküre* is a sacred incest, between two semi-divine personalities, children of the supreme God, Wotan—thus representing the parts of the god which fecundate each other—and it results in the birth of the regenerator of the world, Siegfried.

Shelley, finally, brings the myth down to the wholly human plane; in the "Revolt of Islam," Laon and Cythna, who are also destined to regenerate the world, are an incestuous couple to whom

* *Faërie Queene*, iii., vi.

no more blame is attached than to Wagner's heroes, by which we may see even there a last link with the theme of sacred incest.

Hugo, in a strikingly poetical myth, which is both original and deep, transforms the theme, in *La Fin de Satan*. Satan has a daughter, Liberty, the obvious successor of Milton's Sin. When Satan and his daughter are separated, the world is in a state of chaos and perdition; when they are united, the world is saved and it is the end of Satan transformed. It is certainly Hugo who, with remarkable intelligence and strength of poetic intuition, has extracted from this old myth its most human content, by making it declare that in evil itself there is an element of good, which is liberty. And that brings us to a different subject—Hugo's idea covering the theme of incest and the theme of pursuit. Since in the final union of the two separated parts lies the salvation of the world—one thinks both of Plato's hermaphrodites and of the union of God and the Matrona in the Cabala— the pursuit of the feminine part of the divine male is one of the subjects marked out for our poets. The subject has been dwelt upon in India in the myth of Prajapati and his daughter Ushas, whom he pursues and whom he fecundates, producing all the animal and vegetable species, thus giving life to all creation. It is a subject which has come down into folklore, culminating in innumerable expressions in the popular poetry of all countries;

one of the best known forms is the "Chanson de Magali," in Mistral's *Mireille*.

Milton has described the flight of Sin before the ravisher, laying little stress, however, on this feature. Blake goes fully into the whole subject, gives the myth in its entirety and makes it one of the most richly developed themes in all his poetry. One might even say that if the epics have a subject, that is their subject. We have seen the Demiurges divided—to the horror of the Eternals—for Creation. From each one came forth the male power, the Spectre, and the female power, the Emanation; and the Emanation flees away. The pursuits, the reunions, the struggles, the fecundations of each couple of Zoas, as Blake calls them, fill his epics with infinite variety:

> "But Los saw the Female and pitied;
> He embraced her; she wept, she refused
> In perverse and cruel delight,
> She fled from his arms, yet he followed."*

So does the Spectre of another Zoa, Tharmas, pursue Enion, his Emanation, and all Nature springs from her.

And in Blake, as well as in Hugo and the Cabala, evil in the world, the universal struggle will not cease until the male power overtakes the female power and is harmoniously, once and for all, united to her.

* *Book of Urizen*, vi. See Berger, ch. x. and *passim*.

23

II

In this equation God-Nature we have so far pointed out mainly the avatars of the first term. Let us pass now to the presence and dispersion of God in created beings as seen in the pantheism of the poets.

Most of the poets have accepted as a given fact the transformation of God into Nature. Some of them, however, have been troubled as to the cause and manner of it. Why and how did the infinite become the finite, the perfect the imperfect? To Hugo, creation was in its very essence a limitation, an imperfection necessary to ensure the diversity of beings:

" . . . Sans quoi, sur la même hauteur,
La créature étant égale au créateur,
Cette perfection dans l'infini perdue
Se serait avec lui mêlée et confondue,
Et la création, à force de clarté
En lui serait rentrée et n'aurait pas été."*

In the same way, in Milton, God, in order to create beings, was obliged to sever himself from them, to give Adam freedom:

"he had else been a mere mechanical Adam."†

And Milton adopts, consequently, the Cabalists'

* *Contemplations: Ce que dit la Bouche d'ombre.*
† *Areopagitica.*

24

theory of withdrawal: God withheld his will from a certain part of himself, which became the created world:

"... I uncircumscrib'd myself retire,
    And put not forth my goodness, which is free
To act or not."*

God thus fixed a limit above which a creature may not rise. For Blake there is a limit below which he may not sink. Going back to the Gnostic's conception of the Horos, Blake explains that, in his fall, created being would have reached nothingness.

"The Saviour found the limit of contraction and called it Adam."†

God, thus circumscribed, becomes the World or Nature, which the poets love to place above the gods of established religions, going back, so to speak, to the early adoration of Mother Earth, more ancient and more powerful than all the gods. Curiously enough, Spenser and Hugo, at either end of the line of poets, find similar myths to express this feeling.

In Hugo's *Satyre*, a "scapegrace of a god" provokes Olympus by his depredations. Hercules goes in search of him and brings him to the sacred

* *Paradise Lost*, vii. 170.
† *Vala*, iv. 271. Cf. Berger, pp. 132-136.

mount where, though at first despised, he ends by transforming himself into the whole of Nature, before whom the gods are as nothing. The architecture of the "Mutability Cantos" is very similar; and though at first sight the sense is different, the central idea is the same.

A Titaness, daughter of Earth, disturbs the gods by her ambition and her conquests; Hermes goes in search of her and, although he is unable to compel her to do so, she comes to Olympus, defies the gods and appeals to the supreme power, Nature. The final judgment matters little, the important part being the invocation of Nature who shall judge all the gods:

"This great grandmother of all creatures;"

who could say with the transformed Satyr:

"Place à tout, je suis Pan; Jupiter! à genoux."

Spenser's Jupiter recognises the supreme authority of Nature, saying to her:

"And unto me addoom that is my due;
That is, the rule of all, all being ruled by you."

Spenser had already expressed this feeling of veneration for Mother Earth in his Canto VI of Book III on the Garden of Adonis; there the Sun is the universal Father who fecundates his sister the Earth; whence spring all creatures (stanza 9).

"Great father he of generation
Is rightly called, the author of life and light;
And his fair sister for creation
Ministreth matter fit, which tempred right
With heat and humour breeds the living
        wight."*

And Milton's Satan gives utterance to a very
similar idea: what are the gods, he says, more than
we are? We are the sons of the Earth, not the sons
of the gods:

"The gods are first, and that advantage use
On our belief, that all from them proceeds;
I question it, for this fair Earth I see,
Warmed by the Sun, producing every kind,
Them nothing."†

Likewise, in Shelley's "Prometheus Unbound,"
Prometheus calls to Earth:

"O Mother Earth!"

Earth replies:

"The many children fair
Folded in my sustaining arms; all plants,
And creeping forms, and insects rainbow-winged,
And birds and beasts, and fish, and human shapes,
. . . shall take and interchange sweet nutriment."‡

* Note again here the divine incest.
† *Paradise Lost*, ix. 717.
‡ iii. 3, 84 and foll.

In Wagner, Erda corresponds to a similar conception. Wotan says to her:

> "bekannt ist dir
> was die Tiefe birgt,
> was Berg und Thal,
> Luft und Wasser durchwebt,
> Wo Wesen sind
> weht dein Athem:
> wo Hirne sinnen
> haftet dein Sinn."

The pantheistic feeling in Goethe is at once too well known and expressed in too involved a manner to be dwelt on here.

A conception which is derived straight from this pantheism is the old neo-platonic theory of the scale of beings; it finds a place in nearly all the great poets. Here is an example in Milton:

> "One first matter all,
> Indu'd with various forms, various degrees
> Of substance, and in things that live, of life;
> But more refin'd, more spiritous, and pure.
> As nearer to him plac't or nearer tending . . .
>
> Flowers and their fruits,
> Man's nourishment, by gradual scale sublim'd
> To vital spirits aspire, to animal,
> To intellectual . . .
> Differing but in degree, in kind the same."*

* *Paradise Lost*, v. 473.

And in Hugo:

"Comme sur le versant d'un mont prodigieux
Vaste mêlée aux bruits confus, du fond de l'ombre
Tu vois monter à toi la création sombre.
Le rocher est plus loin, l'animal est plus près.
Comme le faîte altier et vivant, tu parais.
Mais, dis, crois-tu que l'être illogique nous trompe,
L'échelle que tu vois, crois-tu qu'elle se rompe?
. . . non, elle continue, invincible, admirable,
Entre dans l'invisible et dans l'impondérable,
Y disparaît pour toi. . . ."*

### III

Related to this conception of the scale of beings
and proceeding naturally from the feeling for
Mother Earth, we have the feeling of the kinship
of man with the animals—a primitive and innate
feeling shared by nearly all poets. Lamartine
unites the two conceptions very definitely:

"Vous ferez alliance avec les brutes même,
Car Dieu qui les créa veut que l'homme les aime.
D'instinct, d'intelligence à differents degrés
Elles ont eu leur part; vous la reconnaîtrez,
Vous lirez dans leurs yeux, douteuse comme un
    rêve,
L'aube de la raison qui commence et se lève.
Vous n'étoufferez pas cette vague clarté,

* *Contemplations: Ce que dit la Bouche d'ombre.*

29

Présage de lumière et d'immortalité.
Vous la respecterez, car l'ange la respecte;
La chaîne à mille anneaux va de l'homme à
l'insecte,
Que ce soit le premier, le dernier, le milieu,
N'en insultez aucun, car tous tiennent à Dieu."*

Wagner is certainly the poet who has most accurately expressed this primitive feeling of mankind, which is, indisputably, one of the most solid bases of the different forms of totemism. To his descendants and to his enemies the god Wotan identified himself with the wolf: living like a grim recluse and pursued by all in the woods, he took the name of the wolf, as Sigmund relates:

"Wolfe, der war mein Vater."

He adopted also its habits; he hunts and is hunted by men, like a beast.

"Zum Jagen zog
    mit dem Jungen der Alte:
    von Hetze und Harst
    einst kehrten sie heim:
    da lag das Wolfsnest leer;
        lange Jahre
        lebt der Junge
    mit Wolfe im wilden Wald;
        manche Jagd
        ward auf sie gemacht."

* *La chute d'un ange*, Vision viii.

And the god finally disappears, it seems, being killed like a wolf, leaving its skin behind:

> "der Jäger viele
> fielen den Wölfen,
> in Flucht durch den Wald
> trieb sie das Wild;
> Doch ward ich vom Vater versprengt:
> seine Spur verlor ich,
> eines Wolfes Fell
> nur traf ich im Forst."

When Fricka accuses him, she knows how to upbraid him with this animal avatar:

> "jetzt dem Wurfe der Wölfin
> wirfst du zu Füssen dein Weib."

This identification of the god with the ancestor and with the animal is very complete in the *Ring*, and Wotan's descendants retain the characteristics of the clan, incest between the two children of the wolf making its appearance as the inevitable consequence of primitive feelings.

Strange to say, it is a sixteenth-century poet, overflowing with recollections of classical paganism, who has, after Wagner, best depicted this dubious union of man with beast. Spenser, in his Sir Satyrane, gives us a strange compound of human and animal nature, a mixture to which he adds, besides, certain attributes of the Nature divinities. Son of a satyr and brought up in the woods, he has definitely allied himself with the animals, and yet he is noble and upright. Half beast himself, of "beastly kind," he is the lord of wild animals:

"That every beast for fear of him did fly and quake."*

We can only note in passing the existence of this feeling for animals in Whitman. In "Sea Drift, out of the Cradle Endlessly Rocking," Whitman places himself in the soul of a bird which has lost its mate, with a simplicity and power of feeling which is almost more than human, and to him the union of man with animal is not the outcome of man's lower senses, but, on the contrary, of his longing for beauty and eternity. The bird becomes a kind of demon which gives utterance to the deepest and boldest desires of the human soul, and in the dialogue between the man and the bird on the seashore,

"The savage old mother incessantly crying,"

there is a very special essence of equality between them, and both of them commune together as being in some way participators in the divinity of Nature:

"Demon or bird! (said the boy's soul)
Is it indeed towards your mate you sing? or is it
mostly to me?

* *Faërie Queene*, I, vi., st. 21-30.

32

For I, that was a child, my tongue's use sleeping,
Now I have heard you,
Now in a moment I know what I am for—I
    awake."

Similarly, to Nietzsche, the only two companions
of Zarathustra with whom he is really in communion are the eagle and the serpent; similarly,
in Shelley's "Prometheus Unbound" the animals
participate joyously in the universal deliverance
when Jupiter is overthrown; in Milton, on the
other hand, it is the fall of man which involves the
animals also in its consequences, they becoming
mortal as he does. But it is idle to add other evidence of a feeling so widespread among poets,
that in its general expression it is no longer characteristic of any particular conception of life.

To Hugo—and this allows us to pass on to conceptions of immortality often associated in poets
with conceptions of animal kinship—the relations
between man and beast are dominated by the idea
of metempsychosis. A weird feeling of bewilder-
ment seizes him in the presence of animal and
plant life:

"Afrique aux plis infranchissables,
O gouffre d'horizons sinistres, mer des sables,
Sahara, Dahomey, lac Nagaîn, Darfour . . .
Paysages de lune où rôde la chimère,
Où l'orang-outang marche un bâton à la main,
Où la nature est folle et n'a plus rien d'humain";

33

precisely because man loses there the sense of his own identity, and because the orang-outang is a grotesque man, has perhaps been a man or will perhaps become one:

"Oh! si la conjecture antique était fondée,
Si le rêve inquiet des mages de Chaldée,
L'hypothèse qu' Hermès et Pythagore font,
Si ce songe farouche était le vrai profond . . .
O ces êtres affreux dont l'ombre est le repaire,
Ces crânes aplatis de tigre et de vipère,
Ces vils fronts, écrasés par le talon divin,
L'ours, rêveur noir, le singe, effroyable sylvain,
Ciel bleu! s'il était vrai que c'est là ce qu'on
    nomme
Les damnés, expiant d'anciens crimes. . . ."*

Here the poet is in an argumentative mood, he has doubts; but the idea is almost always dormant in his mind, and many of his prose and verse passages which have been termed obscure become clear if we take into account that this is what preoccupied him through all the latter part of his life.† *La Bouche d'ombre* of the *Contemplations* has no doubts:

"Toute faute qu'on fait est un cachot qu'on
    s'ouvre . . .
Tout bandit, quand la mort vient lui toucher
    l'épaule

* *L'art d'être grand-père—le poème du Jardin des Plantes.*
† Particularly in *William Shakespeare.*

34

Et l'éveille, hagard, se retrouve en la geôle
Que lui fit son forfait, derrière lui rampant;
Tibère est un rocher, Séjan dans un serpent."

Spenser also was fascinated by theories of reincarnation, and the Garden of Adonis is the limbo
where souls go to await new reincarnations. "Old
Genius" arranges the manner of their going:

> "such as eternal fate
> Ordained hath, he clothes with sinful mire,
> And sendeth forth to live in mortal state;
> Till they again return back by the hinder gate.
> After that they again returned been,
> They in that garden planted be again . . .
> And then of him are clad with other hue
> And sent into the changeful world again."*

In the same way, Nietzsche has, from his youth
on, toyed with this conception,† and, after all, his
idea of eternal return is pretty closely related to it.
Our poets are all inclined to demand a survival on
or a return to this earth rather than immortality
in another world. Thus Milton, who does not
believe in the existence of the soul, desires the
resurrection of all beings, who are, to him, immortal as a matter of course, and only die in this
world by accident (again a pure conception of the

---

* *Faërie Queene*, iii., vi., st. 32-33.
† See M. Andler's magnificent work, *Nietzsche, sa vie et sa
pensée*, vol. iii., p. 233.

primitives though it has become somewhat complicated), that they may enjoy here a glorious physical and material life.*

IV

The fact is that to nearly all our poets matter is a thing which is good, divine in its essence, since, according to their pantheism, it is part of God himself and sufficient for every manifestation of life and intelligence, "the chief productive stock of every subsequent good," says Milton. Hence a general tendency to what may be called optimistic materialism: the view that matter is good and that the idea of the soul is a useless hypothesis, a doctrine which, says Milton, is contrary to Nature and to Reason. And Nietzsche's Zarathustra delivers two fulminating discourses—"Von den Hinterweltlern " and "Von den Verachtern des Leibes"—against those who look for another world and scorn the human body. It is the same often with Shelley, Goethe and Whitman. All naturally are not materialists, though all, except Blake, have this conception that matter is good. But with all, this tendency complicates their theories of immortality, for the ordinary Christian theory of survival in another world is repugnant to them. In general, they wish to "save the flesh"; they

* Cf. Saurat, *Milton et le Matérialisme*. It is a feeling very prevalent among savages that nothing dies as a matter of course.

have little need for another world; this one is
enough for them.

Let us point out, by the way, in two of them, a
curious reversion to the ancient theory that immortality was not for all men but only for a few
exceptional beings. Goethe conveys this at the
end of Act III of the second *Faust*.

"Wer keinen Namen sich erwarb, noch Edles will,
   Gehört den Elementen an; so fahret hin!"

So does Hugo in the curious passage in *Religions
et Religion*, in which two of Dante's verses dis-
cuss, in the poet's absence, whether they will be
immortal or not. Dante returns, erases one and
retains the other. God does the same with men.*

The being's return to its original elements,
noted in the passage from Goethe, and enlarged
on throughout that part of the second *Faust*, is
met with frequently. Milton speaks of it:

"Every constituent part returns at dissolution
to its elementary principle."†

And Shelley:

"And death shall be the last embrace of her (earth)
   Who takes the life she gave, even as a mother,
   Folding her child, says, 'Leave me not again.' "‡

* *Religions et Religion*, grande édition, Hetzel, p. 246. Cf.
*post scriptum*, p. 188.
   † *Treatise of Christian Doctrine*, Bohn, iv. 279.
   ‡ *Prometheus*, III., iii. 104.

None of our poets naturally accept death as final; nearly all of them see in it an expansion of personality; to almost all, nothing which has been can perish whatever form survival may take. Thus Whitman, in many ways the most modern of all, writes:

"I swear I think now that everything without
    exception has an eternal soul!
The trees have, rooted in the ground! the weeds
    of the sea have, animals!
I swear I think there is nothing but immortality."*

For the inevitable consequence of the pantheistic feeling of universal kinship is immortality for all. Milton, clearly explaining the idea, says:

"If all things are not only from God, but of God, no created thing can be finally annihilated."†

And Blake:

"For everything exists and not one sigh nor
    smile nor tear,
One hair or particle of dust, not one can pass
    away."‡

So we come to the myth which embraces and explains all those transformed and scattered fragments of myths that we have collected; the myth

* *Leaves of Grass*, "To Think of Time," in fine.
† *T.C.D.*, p. 181.
‡ *Jerusalem*, pp. 13, 66.

38

common to almost all poets who have interested themselves in philosophy: the ancient myth of the sacrifice of Prajapati, torn to pieces for creation and made whole again by the ritual of sacrifice, reconstituted also by the evolution of the world, the object of which is to re-create God; or similarly the Orphic myth, or the Osiris myth.

Nietzsche took it straight from the Orphic hymns,* and devoted a part of his life to trying to prove that there lay the meaning of Greek tragedy. A poet's idea when straying into archæology; but also a primitive feeling that the individual is nothing but a member of a group; a consciousness of the collective life that Nietzsche had cultivated in himself. Milton gives a semi-Christian, semi-cabalist form of the theory in his reconstitution of "Greater Man."

Blake says:

"Man looks out in tree and herb and fish and bird
     and beast,
  Collecting up the scattered portions of his im-
     mortal body
  Into the elemental forms of everything that
     grows."†

At the end of *Ce que dit la Bouche d'ombre*, the whole of creation comes at last to re-incorporate itself with God.

* See *Andler*, I. 369, and III. 38.
† *Vala*, viii. 550-573.

"Ainsi que le soleil tire à lui la nuée
　　Et l'emplit d'arcs-en-ciel,
Dieu, de son regard fixe attirant les ténèbres,
Voyant vers lui du fond des cloaques funèbres,
　　Où le mal le pria,
Monter l'énormité bégayant des louanges,
Fera rentrer, parmi les univers archanges,
　　L'univers paria."

To Whitman, the great problem is that of the Identity to be re-established; the reconciliation of the individual "egos" with the total Ego: all his work is built up on this idea, and he himself explains in prose that to prove this is the aim of his poetry.* The final reconstituted Being is Santa Spirita:

"Essence of forms, life of the real identities, permanent, positive, (namely the unseen)
Life of the great round world, the sun and stars and of war,
Of the general soul."†

Everything is preparing for it:

"The exquisite scheme is for it and the nebulous float is for it and the cohering is for it!
And all preparation is for it—and identity is for it—and life and materials are altogether for it!"‡

* *Specimen Days* (Scott), p. 270.
† "The Square Deific."
‡ "To Think of Time."

40

And everything will be found there. Whitman gives us a curious list of all the unnamed lands:

"Of their languages, government, marriage, literature, products, games, wars, manners, crimes, prisons, slaves, heroes, poets, I suspect their results curiously await us in the yet unseen world. I suspect I shall meet them there."*

Also the poet says to all things and persons:

"You furnish your parts towards eternity
  Great or small, you furnish your parts toward the soul."†

V

Having established the more or less common ground of doctrines and myths, I will confine myself to pointing out the community of moral ideas. The primary instrument of this ultimate reconstitution of Unity is, in the majority of cases, the election of a certain number of beings in a further stage of evolution than the others. These beings, conscious of forming parts of God, are freed from the constraint of any moral or other law. We start off, in Milton, from a simple deviation of the traditional idea that to the pure all things are pure: Milton calls that Christian liberty,

* "Unnamed Lands."
† "Crossing Brooklyn Ferry."

and infers from it the suppression, for regenerated or normal man, of all law, religious, political or civil. Blake takes his stand upon a similar conception in order to arrive at the same conclusions. Through Emerson, who removes it from the Christian atmosphere, the theory reaches Whitman who sings the praises of the individual, a law unto himself and free in all his instincts. Another feature of this election is divine inspiration. Milton already divorced it from Christianity by admitting that all great men of all nations, even pagan ones, were inspired of God and were members of Christ. Blake expands the idea without modifying it. But we come across the theory again secularised in Hugo, with his poet-prophets, magi, torch-bearers, interpreters in every case of the divine Spirit. To Hugo, also, liberty is the divine method of suppressing primitive limitation and man progresses towards an increasingly greater freedom from every law. That is, in the main, the meaning of *La Fin de Satan*. Nietzsche unites these two features: the Superman is at once the Inspired One and Free Man and the direct descendant of the Puritan Elect. M. Andler has, besides, brought to light Nietzsche's debt to Emerson, who handed on to him the elements elaborated by Anglo-Saxon puritanism. Wagner has, in Siegfried, his chosen man, the regenerator of the world, the instrument selected by the supreme God. All of which is in harmony with the aim of

Orphism and the mysteries—to make gods—and consequently with the whole collection of traditions we are examining here. Nietzsche even went right back to the original sources in a Dionysian enthusiasm for the pre-Socratics.

From this conception of liberty springs rebellion: nearly all our poets are rebels and incline to amorality and religious or political anarchy. The theme of rebellion against morality, against society, against God is, moreover, poetically rich; but they link it up logically with a general system. Milton's Satan is the first and the greatest rebel in modern literature. Milton condemns him, but he draws him largely from his own feelings. Blake, in his poetry, is the out-and-out rebel. Shelley hymns the dethronement of Jupiter; Wagner the downfall of the gods; Zarathustra is the great destroyer of values and of gods; Hugo devotes his finest epic effort to the revolt of Satan. Whitman embodies in modern humanity the ideal of rebellion against all law, and, in "The Square Deific," he includes in the godhead Satan, to him, as to Hugo, an indispensable element.

In all is asserted the legitimacy of the desires of the body and of matter, over which orthodox religious conceptions kept a strict watch when they did not utterly condemn them, and with all the justification of sensuality is constantly kept in mind.

We have, then, before us, not certainly a co-

43

herent, well-constructed doctrine handed on from one poet to another, but a collection of ill-defined conceptions which yet all belong, so to speak, to the same family of ideas; and this collection is outside the pale of Christianity.

The first natural hypothesis consists in seeing here one of the forms of the evolution of neo-platonism, from the Renaissance to our own day. This hypothesis is not false, but it is inadequate. Neo-platonism has played its part, an important part, in poetry. But a very large number of the conceptions that we have gathered together have their origin elsewhere. Especially is the doctrine of immanence, almost universal among our poets, contrary to neo-platonism, as it is usually understood. Some definite points are on the other hand already established.

Milton made use of *Hermes Trismegistus* and the works of the Cabalists.* Blake was a Swedenborgian; he availed himself of Gnostic notions such as the conception of the Evil Demiurge, and made abundant use of the Cabala.† Goethe turned everything to account: he interested himself in occultism all his life;‡ and was one of the first to become acquainted with the literature of India, which from the end of the eighteenth century, through

* Cf. *Milton et le Matérialisme Chrétien.*

† Cf. B. Fehr, *William Blake und die Kabbala* (Englishe Studien, 1920). M. Berger had already noted the fact. Cf. also Saurat, *Blake and Modern Thought.*

‡ Cf. A. Loiseau, *Goethe,* pp. 100-106.

44

translations, adds its impetus to that of the non-Christian currents anterior to it.

Nietzsche drew his inspiration from Orphism as well as from India.* As to Hugo, he knew India; thus his poem "Suprématie," in *La Légende des Siècles*, treats very definitely, with the same details, the subject of the third part of the "Kenaupanishad." His relations with spiritists, occultists, etc., provide us with some curious data.

Wagner adapted to his philosophy the folklore and the mythology of the North. Whitman, too, after Emerson, steeped himself in translations of Hindu poems.† All these different elements are in general harmony with the neo-platonic influence.

One may say, moreover, speaking generally, that since the Renaissance, with the Italian neo-platonic movement, the publication of the *Hermes Trismegistus*, the publication of the *Zohar*, all these conceptions are in the common domain of the cultured; he who will can adopt them. Once they cast off religious orthodoxy, the poets found themselves face to face with a mass of traditions, incoherent, no doubt, as to detail, but all moving in the same direction: that of a popular pantheism, which had itself survived through the Middle Ages.‡

* Cf. Andler, vol. ii., p. 441.

† See particularly his notes to *Democratic Vistas*.

‡ Cf. Jundt, *Histoire du panthéisme populaire au Moyen Age et au XVIe siècle*, Paris, 1875. See also Mr. H. Murray, *The Witch Cult in Western Europe*, Oxford, 1921.

The historical circumstances which established contact for this or that poet are, no doubt, interesting, but they are of little general importance: the contact was established, in many cases, for authors who did not profit by it and who saw in this mass of ideas and legends only their obvious absurdity. We will leave on one side, then, the question of influences in order to set ourselves a more important problem. Why, generally speaking, did all great poets, interested in ideas, develop in the same way; why did they cling to the same collection of traditions and myths, so that one can, without exaggeration, speak of a doctrine common to philosophical poetry?

This community is much more a community of outlook than a community of ideas. It is striking in some cases in which intercourse is impossible. For instance, M. Berger has very justly pointed out that Hugo, in *La Fin de Satan*, and Blake viewed the French Revolution in a very similar fashion, as a mystical event of importance in the spiritual history of the world.* I have shown how Milton reconstructed a primitive Buddhist myth, which tells how the first-born of the gods made use of his chronological priority to make all the other gods and beings believe that he had created them.†

Finally, and it is in this direction that I see the

---

* In the chapter, "The French Revolution," added to the English edition of his *William Blake*, p. 325.

† *La Pensée de Milton*, pp. 227-228.

solution, M. van Gennep has pointed out incident-
ally that Nietzsche was the culminating point of
ideas derived from the primitives.*

M. Lévy-Bruhl, giving a synthesis of the results
of ethnographical studies, has tried to estimate the
psychology of what he calls the "primitive mentality." Whatever corrections may be necessary
as to the details and as to the focussing of this
conception, it appears to me, in its essence, to be
valid and sound, and to extend far beyond the
psychology of savages. This primitive mentality
seems to me to survive in the midst of our modern
civilisations and to attain in the poets a magnifi-
cence of expression which may hide from us its
identity. The facts studied in the course of this
work arise from this mentality. For beyond neo-
platonism, through "popular pantheism," through
the Cabala, occultism in general, Orphism, the
epics of ancient India, the sagas of the North, our
poets have gone back to the deepest sources of
folklore. The great ideas or feelings which are at
the base of the conceptions that we have collected
here, the adoration of Mother Earth, the sense of
animal kinship, the idea of reincarnation, the
legends of creation by sexual act—these are the
permanent themes—are the ideas and feelings of
the primitives, elaborated, no doubt, in the course
of ages, but remaining fundamentally identical.
The poet is a "primitive." The few general traits

* *Les Rites de passage*, p. 279.

that M. Lévy-Bruhl has tried to delineate in the savage characterise the genus poet throughout all the ages. The fundamental trait is, without doubt, what M. Lévy-Bruhl calls the indifference to secondary causes: the fact that what interests the savage is not so much the immediate and tangible cause of an event as its mystical significance.* The savage does not recognise accident, but looks behind it for the sorcerer or the spirit who has caused it: thus death never seems, to certain peoples, to be a natural thing; it is caused by an intervention of a spiritual nature. Is it not the inevitable tendency of the poetic mind to act in the same way, not to be interested in the direct, physical, secondary, immediate cause of a fact but to find in it a spiritual import? When Shelley thus describes the moon:

"And ever changing, like a joyless eye
    That finds no object worth its constancy . . ."

When Hugo, in the magnificent image which closes "Booz Endormi," wonders with Ruth—

"Quel dieu, quel moissonneur de l'éternel été
    Avait en s'en allant négligemment jeté
    Cette faucille d'or dans le champ des étoiles,"

their minds work like that of the savage; they are looking beyond the physical fact for the spirit which has caused it. Doubtless they do not take

* To employ a convenient term, though it should be used with as much discretion as the word "primitive."

these conceptions seriously, but that is the way
their brain functions; and it makes of their work
poetry as distinct from a rhymed version of what
is merely prose.

I will pass rapidly over other, perhaps less
important, characteristics selected by M. Lévy-
Bruhl, which are equally typical of the poets; the
gregarious sense, which makes them intensely
conscious of the group, the nation and, beyond
that, the earth itself, and of their kinship with all
beings, with nature, with the Cosmos; their indifference to contradictions between different parts
of their conceptions; their power of intuition and
expression: all qualities which make a primitive
of the poet. What primitives have succeeded in
expressing the sufferings of the neglected dead as
Baudelaire has done?

"Les morts, les pauvres morts ont de grandes
douleurs
Et quand octobre souffle, émondeur de vieux
arbres,
Leur vent mélancolique à l'entour de leurs
marbres,
Certe, ils doivent trouver les vivants bien ingrats."

*Ungrateful* because it is the dead who cause the
affairs of the living to prosper, who make their
harvests increase and lead to success their hunting
and their campaigns, and because in return the
living owe gratitude and service to the dead.

49

And what poet-magician of a savage tribe has described better than Verlaine the feelings of the outraged dead and the terrible effects of their anger?

"Les morts que l'on fait saigner dans leur tombe
    Se vengent toujours.
Ils ont leur manière et plaignez qui tombe
    Sous leurs grands coups sourds,
Mieux vaut n'avoir jamais connu la vie,
Mieux vaut la morte lente, d'autres suivie,
Tant le temps est long, tant les coups sont lourds."

Thus the savage will prefer the most certain, imminent dangers, death in the midst of torture, to the danger of arousing the anger of his ancestors by not conforming to some imperious custom of his race or by leaving unfulfilled some necessary rite.*

Possibly, we repeat, the poet does not always believe in these conceptions produced by his purely poetic faculties, and yet does he not arrive at a sort of half-belief in the ardour of his inspiration? But when he is dealing with great philosophical problems, his mind is ever led away by acquired habits into ways of seeing, thinking and feeling which are those of the "primitive mentality." So, however slight the contact established may be—

* Cf. M. Lévy-Bruhl, *La mentalité primitive*, pp. 70, 77, 78, 80 and *passim*. I have chosen, moreover, facts accepted, I think, by all ethnographers.

and we have seen that since the Renaissance such contact is easy—the poet interested in religious philosophy will naturally turn to the conceptions and myths derived from primitive religions of mankind.

There is therefore no need to attach too much importance to the question of influences, which only provide opportunities. The evolution of philosophical poetry becomes the history of the evolution of a certain type of mind—the type opposed to the *scientific* mind, even though there are often strange links between the two—which is yet far from having disappeared from our civilisations. And if its existence is really bound up with that of poetry itself, it is hardly desirable that it should disappear.

For this type of mind Christianity as it stands, after the immense work of logical cogitation done by the Schoolmen, after the Renaissance and the Reformation, is much too civilised a religion; a religion which no longer satisfies, which is even at war with certain of the fundamental needs of the "primitive," which, in any case, does not permit of any roving about in pursuit of obscure, disturbing or alluring myths, and of dim elusive ancestral memories, ever present in the inmost being of poets. This primitive mentality survives, moreover, in the common people, especially in the peasant class. And where is there a poet who, in going back a few generations, finds no peasants among his ancestors?

51

From this central point of psychology, it can be seen how useful the history of religions may be to literary criticism. Poets like Hugo or Nietzsche, who are explained neither by the evolution of literary ideas nor by that of philosophical ideas, are put in their proper places in known currents, which have come down from remotest antiquity and may also be studied among contemporary non-civilised people, currents which become, so to speak, subterranean in our civilised societies, but make their presence manifest in the vagaries of occultism and sometimes in the most sublime poetry.*

## II. THE PSYCHOLOGICAL BASIS

### SENSUALITY AND PRIDE

Is it possible to find a formula which will allow us to classify under one head these intellectual phenomena from the savage to the modern poet? Perhaps, widely interpreted, the ideas sociology has circulated would give us a basis—a working hypothesis—which is at least apparently sound. One may consider that from a certain point of view

* M. van Gennep has expressed ideas parallel to these, on the survival in civilised societies of primitive feelings, notably that of animal kinship, in *L'état actuel du problème totémique*, p. 348. I attach great importance to this confirmation of the ideas developed here.

(which I do not claim to be the only one to hold) man is, first of all, the instrument of a group. His mind is thus the individual and fragmentary process by which the group arrives at the consciousness of itself. Man is a *social being*, but the "Society" of which he is a part does not include only men. He is one with the entire Universe; he is subject to the influence of all the members of the Universe who are near him, of men, of course, but also, and especially in the beginning of the race at any rate, of the forests, caverns and mountains in which he lives, of the animals who are his companions, his prey or his enemies. It is, in the first place, a physical influence, but also, and especially in the beginning, a psychological influence, ill determined but tremendous, often an influence which takes complete possession of him. Whatever may be the possible definition of totemism, if ever the ethnographers come to an agreement about it, there emerges, from the multitude of facts grouped under that name, this one fact—that primitive man frequently submitted himself consciously to this influence, that in his totemic ceremonies he turns himself into, *he is*, the animal or the plant he represents, in a sort of desperate attempt to get back into the animal or plant world of which he feels himself part. He tries to express the group consciousness, a consciousness which he feels powerfully yet uncertainly overflowing from humanity upon nature.

The poet is equally the instrument of a group, of the social group in which he lives—that is a commonplace—and of the *natural* group also. M. Cazamian has given us on this subject a very detailed study—"L'intuition panthéiste chez les romantiques anglais"*—which it is useless to do all over again and which I will content myself with using. After studying closely five or six early nineteenth century poets, he comes to the conclusion that the poets accepted the ideas of a traditional logical or mystical pantheism because their sensibility had prepared them for it. The real origin of their ideas lies in their intuition. Analysing this intuition, M. Cazamian finds at the root of it physiological effects of nature on the nerves of the poet, clearly related to sensuality; but other elements, harder to specify, act on the conscious or the subconscious, leading to the perception of the life diffused in nature, to the creation of myths which fill the elements, plants, all beings and things with anthropomorphic forces. The poet then feels nature in the same way as did the primitive; he lets it, so to speak, express itself in him. Hence the fundamental likeness between their conceptions; and when the poets turn their attention to philosophy, they merely translate these manifestations of sensibility into intellectual language.

M. Cazamian has analysed only one side of the

* L .Cazamian, *Etudes de psychologie littéraire*. Payot, 1913.

poetic mind, the external side, but one can go further than this; to this external intuition there corresponds an internal intuition. M. Cazamian points out the general state of euphory that nature produces in the poet. The poet puts himself in tune with the sphere of his sensibility, he feels nature, but at the same time he feels his own self with a like intensity; his consciousness of his own individuality increases with his consciousness of the entire creation, and even though it be only to sink his own individuality in nature, he feels, in the first place, his own individuality more deeply. M. Cazamian has noted the relation between the intuition of nature and sensuality; let us add to that, as corresponding to internal intuition, pride. Pride is often almost a purely physical feeling, an exaltation of physiological life itself, that is found in animals. And if the great philosophical poets, Milton, Blake, Whitman, Shelley, Goethe, were full of sensuality, they were equally full of pride. And just as their sensuality (in the broad sense) led them to identify themselves with nature, their pride led them to identify themselves with God, thus building up their pantheism on a double sentimental basis, on a double intuition, external and internal.

We are then face to face with a psychological type within fairly wide yet well-defined limits, with natures both proud and sensual; with minds intensely sensitive to variations of internal or

external circumstances; with a way of conceiving
and representing life which is, in its essence, that
of the primitive.

It is important from the beginning to distin-
guish this type from another which seems at times
rather akin to it: the mystical type. In order to
give an exact meaning to this word "mystical,"
let us follow M. Delacroix's *Etudes d'Histoire
et de Psychologie du Mysticisme:* it will appear
to us then that our philosophical poets are not
mystics. This designation cannot be applied to
Spenser or Milton or Whitman, or any of the
others except in a rather special sense to Hugo.
Blake himself is not, properly speaking, a mystic:
he is only a visionary. Firstly, in most of the poets
sensuality has free rein, while in the mystics it is
carefully bridled.* Moreover, the pride which is
characteristic of our poets is quite incompatible
with the abdication of personality, the incorpora-
tion in God, which is perhaps the most persistent
feature of mysticism. The feeling of love for God
himself does not exist in our poets. Milton speaks
of the deity with peculiar coldness, like a pure
intellectual; with most of the others the occasion
even for this feeling of love does not exist. God
as a personality capable of being loved no longer
enters into their conceptions.

Finally, while the mystics are above all senti-

* It has even been suggested that the "cause" of mysticism
lies in this suppressed sensuality.

56

mentalists and generally mediocre as regards in-
tellect, the philosophical poets are intellectuals in
their own particular way: great lovers of debate,
great masters of logical subtleties, rationalists to
the very core.

M. Delacroix concludes: "The states of the
mystics must be placed among the exalted states
of what we may term the unprecise series of
psychological states." The philosophical poets, on
the contrary, belong to the category of clear
thinkers. Blake again is only an apparent exception; his obscurity is not due to the vagueness of
his ideas or perceptions, but to the wilful confusion
of his symbols. When he can be caught saying
what he thinks, he is very logical and clear.

Now that these fundamental differences are
established, let us review the points of contact.
The philosophical poets often made use of mystic
doctrines, seized hold, here and there, of fragments of the teachings of the schools or authors
of mysticism. But these were never more to them
than material which they used with a different
significance, making it as a rule serve theories
which are altogether rational. M. Berger has shown
in his study of Blake that there is a kind of antagon-
ism between poetry and mysticism and that Blake's
increasing mysticism ended by destroying the poet
and perhaps even the writer in him.

The philosophical poet is, then, quite an exceptional type; specially characterised by peculiar

intuitions and strength of individuality. His intuitions and inspirations do not come within the category of mysticism but rather within the category of literature. The philosophical poets are before everything else poets—a great part of their works is pure poetry—but among the poets they are distinguished by the fact that they are interested in ideas. They bring to the contemplation of ideas the forms and habits of the poetic mind, and a nature in which the trait of pride in particular is perhaps more strongly marked than in the majority of the other poets.

## III. THE QUESTION OF SOURCES

This necessarily rather broad definition of the mind of a philosophical poet allows us to take up a definite position on the question of sources. No doubt it is sometimes possible to indicate exactly the author or the book from which one of our poets takes his ideas. From long before the Renaissance nearly all the ideas that we are concerned with existed in the intellectual atmosphere of cultured Europe; even when we recognise a case of direct transmission from one author to another, it is as well to consider the direct transmission only as accidental: communication could have been established in a thousand other ways with almost similar results. What is much more important is the receptivity of the poet, his predispositions; because of this, writers of the same intellectual type receive similar ideas, even if they have not access to the same sources.

Ideas are the microbes of the moral world. They swarm and reproduce with disconcerting rapidity. The conditions they engender are contagious and their propagation depends on the state of the organism receiving them, which can eliminate them or can let itself be invaded by them. They pass from one to another by ways often unsuspected; they are in the air just as much as microbes. They flourish everywhere where character, surroundings, society are favourable to them. Philosophers isolate them in bacterial cultures as it were, seeking means to cultivate them or to destroy them, creating surroundings favourable or unfavourable to their development. But the activities of philosophers no more explain the propagation of ideas than the activities of doctors the growth of epidemics. Ideas circulate in the world almost independently of individuals; their rôle in history does not depend so much on the men who officially represent them as on the extent of their hold on the masses. Movements such as Christianity or, nearer to us and very near to our philosophical poets, historically speaking, Bolshevism have often spread among the masses without the guidance of any man of remarkable intelligence. There can be here no consideration of the "truth" of these ideas; a difficult matter to decide or even define without reference to some metaphysical system; one ought rather to speak of their "morality," of the influence they can exercise on the societies in which they are spreading.

My aim, then, is not so much to determine sources, although where that is possible the greatest interest attaches to this investigation, as to indicate currents or zones of ideas. In most cases the ideas exist around, outside, above the authors, who, at a certain stage of their development, lay themselves open to receive them, often by ways or means which are within easy reach of all, but which other authors do not seize because these ideas do not attract them; by bad translations, vague rumours, conversations with men intellectually insignificant. I do not mean here to assert that Blake's ideas are derived from Milton, or that Shelley's or Whitman's are, nor to try to discover a sort of filiation—as from father to son—which would culminate in Goethe, Nietzsche, Hugo. Each of these poets may have known his predecessors and been inspired by them to a certain extent. But in the main we are not concerned with personal influences but with a great general movement, extending from the Renaissance to our own days, which may be called modern pantheism, and which is manifested in each of these great poets. That is why there is little to be gained by studying all the secondary poets who come under the influence of this movement. Let us examine closely the masters; the satellites, except in particular cases where they are of use to us as symptoms, have only very little to teach us. But every time a current of ideas has taken possession of a great mind, a moment of humanity has been expressed. The principal vehicle of the propagation of ideas which have ended by expressing themselves artistically in philosophical poetry is that rather incoherent aggregate which we call occultism. Throughout the whole of these studies we shall have to deal with occultists. Let us try, therefore, from the beginning, to make our meaning clear about them. The philosophical poets, generally speaking (we shall have to consider Blake separately), are not occultists: they are not affiliated to any more or less secret society which could furnish them with their ideas ready-made. But all are acquainted with occultism and make use of it: they all take from it, at different epochs, metaphysical ideas, moral conceptions and above all myths. There are three great reasons for this. First of all, the "primitive" type of mind that we have attributed to the philosophical poets is the same type as that which, diffused among the masses, encourages occultism to flourish there. We shall see the survival, in occult doctrines, of the most "primitive" conceptions of humanity. Therefore our poets are in constant sympathy with the occultist societies of their time. If they are not occultists themselves, it is mainly because of their superior culture: refined by contact with the classics, enamoured of an ideal of art and enlightenment, they are repelled by the dim and doubtful element which plays an important part in occultism, by the dark intricate details of the doctrines which obstinately refuse to lend themselves to poetry.

However, and this is the second reason why occultism attracts them, they find in it an almost inexhaustible mine of new material. Occultism is the place of refuge of all vanquished religions and philosophies. It contains, for the poets, in contrast to the orthodox culture of their time, a whole world of artistic possibilities. There, they find, still living in the fervour of the initiated, deep and ancient myths hardly touched by the majority of poets, and therefore doubly precious.

Finally, we shall see that most of our poets, when they carry their feelings and their conceptions to extremes, are rebels against Christianity.* Here, again, they find themselves in sympathy with occultism which is a world of intellectual rebels. For, after some wavering (as when at the Renaissance Pic de la Mirandole and Reuchlin, and a few popes perhaps, wished to make use of the Cabala to justify Christianity—a chivalrous but foolhardy enterprise), strife has been the normal state of affairs between occultism and

* M. Cazamian has pointed out this trait, op. cit., p. 80.

orthodoxy from the seventeenth century to our own day.

In addition to the intellectual cultural reason which has kept the philosophical poets from foundering in occultist digressions, another reason for their detachment must be noted. Intellectual pride, the existence of which we have proved in all, hindered them from surrendering. They all have the tendency to *fara de se*, the need for intellectual freedom and confidence in one's own mind which are among the traits of modern man. So they made use of the very tempting material of occultism without subjugating themselves to the schools. Even Blake, the worst sufferer from this malady, reconstructed an occult system for himself alone—which is indeed the acme of occultism and which will probably always prevent us from completely understanding him. He combined together, as his fancy dictated, fragments of different traditions and initiations. He did not let any particular school impose its ideas upon him. The philosophical poets are by their nature destined to remain heretics even in the bosom of heresy. and consequently independents.

Having thus noted the relations between our poets and the occultists, we shall be able to make use of the latter and establish pretty accurately their function as vehicles or revealers. Let us note now the relations that hold good for the whole series.

63

The neo-platonism of the Renaissance has been studied so often that I have no wish to engage in this vain task; nor would it serve any great purpose here. There is a misunderstanding between neo-platonism on the one hand and poets like Spenser and Milton on the other. The general scheme of ideas is the same, but the importance attached to facts and conceptions is different. To neo-platonism, matter is bad, together with everything that is composed of it. To our poets, notwithstanding all their varying points of view, matter is, in general, essentially good. No doubt, to many of the neo-platonists of the Renaissance, matter is equally good. But in that case they have been subject to other influences than those of ancient neo-platonism. In spite of their great desire to attach themselves to the school of Plotinus, they are not wholly successful in doing so. They modify the teaching of the master. They adapt it to Christianity, to the intellectual currents of the fifteenth or sixteenth century and to their individual natures. In fact, they adopt the accoutrements of the system but not its spirit.

This condemnation of matter and the flesh, which is inherent in the very essence of the neo-platonic tradition, was never accepted by Judaism; and when the men of the fifteenth or sixteenth century reaffirmed the sanctity of this world which is the vestment and the glory of God, they found that, like Pic de la Mirandole in the *Hepta-*

*plus* and all those who followed him, they had approached certain Jewish states of mind. They joined forces with the Cabala. The intellectual life of cultured Europeans was to some extent pervaded by an enormous mass of occult traditions whose general spirit was similar to that of the Renaissance in its categorical refusal to see evil in matter in itself, and some, at least, of whose fundamental doctrines were easy to reconcile with the aspects of neo-platonism which had attracted the scholars.

To the Renaissance, occultism was the Cabala on the one side and the hermetic books on the other. And there is no doubt that it is from one or the other, and often from one and the other, that the philosophical poets drew whatever was not original in their conceptions. We shall see that each in his turn, Spenser, Milton and later Blake, borrows from these traditions. But they did not absorb the whole of the Cabala nor the whole of the hermetic doctrines. Each took from them only what was useful to him as nourishment. Therefore, a study of the Cabala in itself, or of the hermetic books in themselves, is useless and even misleading, since it would involve us in a protracted analysis of conceptions of which our poets did not avail themselves. For, in point of fact, they adopted only a fairly small number of occultist doctrines. From this small number they sometimes constructed their whole philosophy;

and sometimes they amalgamated the doctrines more or less happily with their orthodoxies.

And if they did not entirely adopt the Cabala or the *Hermes* it is because considerable portions of these compendiums of secret doctrines are not in harmony with the European mind. So in order to place the intellectual current which has influenced modern philosophical poetry the most I will adopt a double proceeding: I will first of all take an authorised witness of contemporary occultism, Madame Blavatsky, almost all of whose doctrine is to be found in fragments here and there in our poets, because, in spite of some appearances to the contrary, she had a modern mind, in many respects a mind belonging to the close of the eighteenth century. Therefore, the choice she made in occultist doctrines is a modern choice, which is in agreement with that of the poets. This landmark being set up at the close of the period under examination, I will try, in order to set up other landmarks at the beginning of that period, to pick out the essential passages from the *Zohar* and from the *Hermes Trismegistus*. This will give us the popularised expression at the Renaissance of the doctrines with which we have to deal.

37222

# III

# OCCULTISM AND LITERATURE

## I. MADAME BLAVATSKY

I HAVE picked out first of all in Madame Blavatsky's colossal work the various features of the synthesis of occultism which she popularised at the end of the nineteenth century under the name of Theosophy. Her chief book, *The Secret Doctrine*, published in English in 1888, is a kind of modern summary of occultism which made use of the data found in all works of this sort since the Renaissance. A kind of Indian veneer has been laid over the structure, but in its materials and build it is European. It is to Fludd, d'Espagnet, Court de Gebelin, Bailly, Fabre d'Olivet, Eliphas Lévi that the ideas expressed by Madame Blavatsky belong, and their origin further back lies in the occultism of the Renaissance. Her infatuation for India is only a fashion, which had doubtless persisted in Russia from the end of the eighteenth century: it is the premature knowledge of Gebelin, Bailly and Voltaire, it is the same inclination towards great theories of civilisations and races. I imagine Madame Blavatsky in her unhappy youth, in the depths of the Russian country, shut up in the castle of one of those nobles of the time of Catherine II, who had collected for himself vast libraries of French works published between 1750 and 1800. In such a retreat this effervescent brain was able to formulate its doctrine at leisure, and to acquire that passion for things Indian which had raged in Europe at that time. A certain amount of travelling in the East must have enabled her to convince herself of the identity of this doctrine of visionary encyclopædists with Indian ideas; if one is looking for them, the resemblances are striking, and we shall see our poets from Blake to Whitman following the same path. In any case the theosophical synthesis allows us to compare the ideas of our philosophical poets with a complete doctrine. This procedure has the advantage of giving us as evidence not a synthesis made *in abstracto* by a scientific mind but a living and fairly widespread religious system.

Occult traditions had for Madame Blavatsky the same fascination as for the poets. But whereas they were in the main only seeking material for their own creations, conceptions to make use of with an artistic or at least intensely personal object in view, Madame Blavatsky, heedless of the form, the verisimilitude, or the effect produced on the cultured reader, was concerned with the collection and organisation of occult doctrines solely for their own sake. For the public of disciples she had in mind the doctrine alone sufficed, art did not exist.

Madame Blavatsky's work thus gives us the rough material of modern occultism and allows us to come to a kind of experimental conclusion about what has really survived in European minds after several centuries of trituration of the ideas of the cabalists and hermetists of the Middle Ages and the Renaissance.

Therefore we have in Madame Blavatsky a precious witness: she gives us in a genuinely rough state the only material in the great occultist quarry which was capable of being worked by the poets. What she rejected was, no doubt, almost totally impossible for the modern mind to assimilate.

The comparison, if one may now and again stretch the ideas under consideration, results approximately in the table given overleaf.*

To make it easier to understand, I will give a brief outline of the doctrine, omitting the particulars which are not to be found in the poets.

God is the noumenon: unfathomable, intangible. His first manifestation is both male and female. God is then, in his expression, a sort of cosmic hermaphrodite, who divides himself into twin powers. These, through the one fecundating the

* In the case of Egypt, India and Greece, I have put into the table only facts easily ascertained and accessible in texts either classic or (in the case of India) known in the nineteenth century. We are not discussing here the Egyptian, Indian or Greek ideas, but the knowledge of such ideas that the poets may have had. With regard to folklore, the situation is quite different, as I explained above.

| | Blavatsky | Folk lore | Egypt | India | Ancient Greece | Neo-Plato | Hermes | Bible (Judaism) | Zohar | Spenser | Milton | Blake | Shelley (Wordsworth) | Emerson | Whit-man | Goethe | Wagner | Nietzsche | Hugo Lamartine Vigny |
|---|---|---|---|---|---|---|---|---|---|---|---|---|---|---|---|---|---|---|---|
| Noumenon God | | • | • | • | | • | • | • | • | | | • | • | • | • | • | | | • |
| Hermaphrodite {divine | | • | • | • | | | • | • | • | | • | • | • | | | | • | | • |
| {human | | | | | | | | | | | • | • | | | | | | | • |
| Incest | | • | | • | | | • | • | • | | • | • | • | | | | | • | • |
| Logos: emanations | | • | | • | • | • | • | • | • | • | • | • | • | • | • | • | | • | • |
| God—Cosmos | | • | | | • | | • | • | • | | • | • | • | • | • | • | • | • | • |
| Divine Matter-Substance | | | | • | • | | • | • | • | | • | • | | • | • | | | • | • |
| Fall: Creation | | • | | • | • | | • | • | • | | • | • | | • | • | • | • | | • |
| Failure of First Creations | | | | • | • | | • | • | | | | • | | | | | | | • |
| The First Races | | | | | • | | • | • | | | • | • | | | | | | | • |
| Incarnation of the Higher Ones | | | | | • | | • | • | • | | • | • | | | | | | | • |
| Mineral-plant Kinship | | • | | • | • | • | | • | | | | • | | | | | | | |
| Animal Kinship | | • | • | • | • | • | • | | • | | | • | | | | | • | | • |
| Multiple Falls | | • | | | • | • | • | | | | • | • | | | | | • | • | |
| The Non-Mental | | • | | | • | • | | | | • | • | • | | | | | | | |
| The Division into Sexes | | • | | • | • | | • | | • | | • | • | • | | | | | | • |
| Advantages of the Fall | | | | | | | | | | | • | • | • | | | | • | • | |
| Reincarnation | | • | • | • | • | • | • | • | • | | • | • | • | • | • | • | • | • | • |
| Cycles and Returns | | • | | | • | | • | | • | • | • | • | • | • | • | | • | • | • |
| Eternal Plans: Fate | | | | • | | • | | • | | | | • | | | • | | | | • |
| Elements 3, 4, 7, 10, etc. | | | | | • | • | | • | | • | • | • | | • | • | • | • | • | |
| Macro and Microcosm | | | | | • | • | • | • | • | • | • | • | • | | • | | • | • | • |
| Sensuality—Woman | | • | | | | | | | | | | • | • | | • | | • | | • |
| Reason and Passion | | | | | • | | • | • | • | | • | • | • | • | • | • | • | • | • |
| Normal Immortality | | • | | | | | | | | | | • | | | • | | | | |
| Desire and Matter Good | | • | | | • | | • | • | • | | • | • | • | • | • | • | • | • | • |
| The Elect: Liberty | | | | | | • | | | | | | • | | • | | | | | |
| The Regeneration: The Total Man or Unique Being | | | | | • | | • | • | • | | • | • | • | • | • | • | • | • | • |

other, produce the world. This is the sacred incest, sometimes divine, sometimes human, which is at the root of numerous myths and primitive or ancient practices. In the abstract, this myth is interpreted by a series of emanations and subdivisions which transform God into a world. This world is made of a material which is none other than the divine substance.

The creation is, from a certain point of view, a fall, a degradation. It was preceded by unsuccessful attempts at creation, of which a few fragments remain in the present creation. There were before our human race other races, inadequate for the fulfilment of the purposes of God, who were destroyed. Certain higher spirits, however, sacrificed themselves and became incarnate among the pre-human races, some of which were, in various respects, preferable to our own race. All beings, moreover, from the mineral creation, plants and animals upwards, are theoretically akin. Certain animals are pre-human, others are the results of various falls. Certain races, such as the "non-mental," reached a very high moral level, while their intelligence was very little developed.

But the chief fall of humanity is associated with the division of the sexes. The first races were a-sexual; then came hermaphrodite races. The division into two sexes took place in degradation and is the origin of present mankind. To the fall, however, certain advantages are attached, especially as regards the development of the "scientific" intelligence.

Among the human races (or sub-races) which preceded ours, the most important are the Lemurians, who inhabited the sunk continent of the South Pacific, and the Atlantis of the vanished Atlantic continent. Each soul must pass successively through all the races which are arranged in a kind of double ladder, up and down, "spirituality" and "intelligence" varying, at the beginning at least, in inverse ratio to each other, so that the higher one is spiritually the less intelligent one is. But at the close of evolution the two qualities will amalgamate. Thus successive reincarnations bring a being through all the races of the world, then through the different worlds and cycles of the universe. These variations take place in pursuance of very definitely fixed eternal plans, and under the direction of higher intelligences who are at a further stage of evolution than man.

Man is composed of a certain number of bodies (or souls) contained within each other, which are not all equally affected by death. This composition is the image of the composition of the universe: the microcosm corresponds to the macrocosm.

Man being made of a divine substance, his desires are sacred and sensuality in particular is legitimate.* The place of woman is very high spirit-

* Madame Blavatsky is, however, rather reserved on this point and blames the Jewish Cabala, which is one of her in-

ually and the reincarnations take little account of changes of sex, trifling operations easily, or at least frequently, brought about. Desire and matter are good in themselves, but reason must dominate passion which becomes holy when thus approved. Immortality is a normal and natural thing for everyone. But certain beings in the course of evolution reach a higher stage than all other souls, and for these the moral law ceases to exist.

Evolution makes souls remount the steps that their falls caused them to descend, and ends by re-incorporating them with the original essence. Thus divine Unity destroyed by creation—for an existent though vague purpose, probably a purpose of expression—is reconstituted. The unique Being thus passes for ever through periods of disintegration and re-integration, expansion and contraction, sleeping and waking, inhaling and exhaling.

tellectual guides, for its tendency to emphasise the sexual side. She accuses the Jews of being extraordinarily sensual; it is true that she had personal reasons for wishing to appear puritanical, accusations of looseness being rife about her.

## II. THE CABALA

The Cabala is the principal current of all this
system of parallel connected rivers. It cannot
certainly be maintained that all our poets borrowed
straight from the Cabala. But even when they
borrowed elsewhere, the traditions which reached
them were either the offspring or poor, and sometimes rather despised, relations of the Cabala. In
volume alone the Cabala constitutes a mass of
traditions so very much more considerable than
the rival schools or their offshoots that it represents, so to speak, the orthodoxy of occultism.
Moreover, at the time of the Renaissance and
during the centuries which followed, the Cabala
impresses European minds through something of a
misunderstanding. It attracts Christians because it
is a current springing directly from the Old Testament, because it is a commentary made by the
chosen people of the sacred books given to the
chosen people; and, with the approval of some of
the popes themselves, this commentary came to
have the reputation of being favourable to the
ideas of Christianity. On the other hand, the
Cabala can be of equal service to the enemies of
Christianity; they find in it the true explanation
of the Bible doctrines of which Christianity is
only a perversion. By its authority as by its volume
the Cabala compels our attention more than any
other system.

Let us here insist once again on the fact that we are not seeking a source so much as a witness. Our poets were not, properly speaking, cabalists any more than they were hermetists or members of any of the other kindred systems—followers of Boehme, Swedenborg, de Saint-Martin or Blavatsky. In most cases the ideas under consideration here must have reached our poets through conversations rather than through reading. And the *Zohar*, constructed in a conversational form, gives us, so to speak, set down on paper the ideal type of our real tradition. So for the expression of occult doctrines we will keep principally to the *Zohar*. We find there the very substance of what, in a more or less diluted form, reached all our poets.*

I do not claim to give here a dogmatic account of the Cabala. No one has the authority to give such an account. There are so many cabalistic schools at war with each other that there is hardly a single point which might not be contested.

I aim only at presenting the ideas and the passages which have seemed to me to be of greatest importance in the history of poetry or perhaps of literature in general. Therefore I have classified these extracts according to the four great themes which are most frequently to be found in the poets.

* The extracts which follow are taken from the French translation of the *Zohar*, by Jean de Pauly, published by M. Lafuma. Leroux. Paris, 1906-1911.

1. The idea that God is an inaccessible power, and yet also the universal matter of which the world is made.

2. The conception of the sexual law according to which all existence is both male and female.

3. The idea that in God and in every category of beings there is an evil side.

4. Theories of reincarnation.

The various abstruse systems resulting from cabalist speculations, such as the organisation of the ten Sephiroth, do not seem to me to have much influenced the great poets. They contained notions too intricate for poetry; and it is rather general theories, ideas which, though vague, are yet in harmony with poetic sensibility, that are to be found in the poets.

Therefore I have put aside all this abstruse speculative element. I have confined myself closely to the primitive element which seems to me to constitute the prime basis of the Cabala, and which lives in exactly the kind of sensibility and thought in which the poets' imaginations play.

As a résumé of the whole, the table that we have just made up shows that, in the main, the statement of Madame Blavatsky's doctrine is a modern statement of the Cabala, a little systematised and strained in this or that direction, but nevertheless correct in its general trend.

76

I shall content myself then, while presenting what seem to me the chief passages from the *Zohar*, with contributing only the most indispensable explanations.

## [A] GOD THE UNKNOWN

*1. The Unfathomable God.  2. The withdrawal.  3. Light as substance and the formation of souls.  4. Light as seed.  5. The responsibility of all beings.  6. The forbidden mysteries.*

### 1. *The Unfathomable God*

God is incomprehensible, being beyond the world and consequently beyond the reach of human thought.

There you will learn that the mysterious Ancient One, after whom all eternally seek, has created that. And who is he?—"Mi" (who). It is he who is called on high the "Extremity of the heavens," for all is in his power. And it is because all seek after him eternally, because his ways are mysterious and because he does not reveal himself that he is called "Mi" (who); and further none must seek to penetrate. This *higher* Extremity of the heavens is called "Mi" (who). But there is another extremity below called "Ma" (what). What difference is there between the one and the other? The first mysterious one, called "Mi," is the one after whom all seek; and after man has sought, after he has striven to ponder and to mount step by step to the last one, at length he reaches "Ma" (what). What hast thou learnt? What hast thou understood? What hast thou sought? For all is as mysterious as before.   [Vol. I., p. 6.]

Still more incomprehensible to us than the world is the thought of God, his object in creating the world; the thought of God is, in essence, the noumenal world, in which, however, the only realities exist.

It is written: "Above the head of the 'Hayoth' is seen a firmament like unto a dazzling crystal, terrible to see"; it is the higher firmament above which none can see *because all that is there* passes understanding. Why? Because all is enveloped in the Thought, and the Thought of the Holy One, blessed be his name, is hidden, secret and *too* exalted for man's understanding to reach and comprehend. *Then*, if the things depending from the supreme Thought are inaccessible, all the more so is the Thought itself. Within the Thought there is none that can comprehend aright; so much the more is it impossible to know the Infinite (ayn-Soph) who is impalpable; vain are all questionings and all ponderings which seek to grasp the essence of the supreme Thought, centre of all, secret of all secrets, without beginning and without end, infinite, of whom but a particle of light is seen, like unto the point of a needle, and *yet* this particle is only visible by reason of the *material* form that it has taken; for the Verb has taken the form of the signs of the alphabet, all of which emanate from the supreme Point.     [Vol. I., p. 129.]

In order to bring about Creation, the inaccessible Verb transformed itself into a central point, that in some incomprehensible way reflects God, whence emanates the light which, by fading, thickening, contracting, whatever may be the metaphor employed, forms the worlds.

78

# GOD THE UNKNOWN

God represents the Central Point, Cause of all things, which remains hidden from all the worlds, which is unknown and which will remain eternally unknown; this is the supreme mystery of the Infinite. From this mysterious Point there issues a slender ray of light which, although likewise hidden and invisible, contains all lights. This slender ray of light receives the vibrations of Him who does not vibrate, *of the mysterious Point*, and reflects the light of Him who sheds no light, *the mysterious Point*. The vibrations felt by the slender ray form around it luminous waves; and this light caused by the waves constitutes the "Spell of spells," *that is to say—the slender ray of light constitutes the spell of the mysterious Point and the light of the waves constitutes the spell of the slender ray of light*. The light caused by the waves contains six signs known only to the slender ray hidden in the centre of this great light.

[Vol. IV., p. 5.]

In this way the slender ray gives birth to a world of light caused by the waves; which world gives light to all the other worlds. Here are some details as to the way in which the Point is formed. The aim of these conceptions is to remove this world as far as possible from God, while still retaining the fact that God is the substance of the world.

The Supreme Point produces a light which diffuses itself in four directions passing through the four doors aforesaid. No creature can bear the brightness of this supreme light. The "Supreme Point" can be seen only by the luminous rays which issue from it. But as all creatures feel an irresistible need to approach the Supreme Point, as a starving man hungers for food, the rays issuing from the "Supreme Point" form at their lower extremities another Point; this is the "Point below." The "Point

79

below" is Elohim; and yet it is the same light as above, the Infinite. This mystery is known to the initiated. The "river which flows out of Eden" denotes the rays uniting the "Point above" to the "Point below." Souls emanate from the "Point above," and are borne by the river to the paradise below (211). From thence they descend into this world where they acquire merit; and from here they return whence they emanate.                    [Vol. IV., p. 219.]

Souls are, then, particles of the divine essence; but it is not only souls that are made from it; the material world is also formed from it, and here we have the birth of the elements.

The white Head wished to glorify his Name; it caused to issue from the primary light a spark which was diffused in three hundred and seventy directions. From this spark issued a pure and buoyant air. In the middle of this air rose a powerful head which spread itself out in the four directions of the world. Thus, this pure air, formed of the spark, surrounds the Head, but it is the most hidden of the Ancient of Days. This air is surrounded by fire and air; the pure air lies above the fire and the ordinary air. The fire in question here is not an ordinary fire, but the fire with which the air is charged and which gives light to two hundred and seventy worlds; it is a fire of justice and that is why the Head bears the name of "powerful Head"; it embraces nine thousand, ten thousand worlds, all surrounded and held up by the pure air. [Vol. V., p. 356.]

We find summed up in the following passages the cabalistic conceptions of the relations between the created and the uncreated, of the power of God before the creation and his part in the creation.

As this supreme light is separated by the curtain drawn between the world above and the world below, it follows that this light appears in two different aspects, being more dazzling above, less transparent below. And as, on the other hand, this same light appears above in the three aspects of "Jehovah Elo Henou Jehovah," the result is that the supreme light appears in six different aspects: three above and three below. Such is the meaning of the word "Bereschitch" which, divided, gives the words 'Bara" "Schitch" (created six); this is an allusion to the curtain drawn between the world above and the one below, which brings up the three varieties of the supreme light to six. The transparency of this curtain is not the same for everyone, nor at all periods of the year; it is at its most transparent during the days intervening between the first day of the year and the Feast of Tabernacles.

[Vol. IV., p. 318.]

The Creation came about through the will of the mysterious Infinite. Only for the creation of the details of the work was the term "word" uttered *for the first time*, as it is written: "And Elohim said: 'Let there be light.'" *Thus* the Verb appears only for the creation of details, while the creation of the *general matter* came about before the manifestation of the Verb. That is why in the two first verses of Genesis, *in which the creation of general matter* is related, the word "vayomer" (said) is not found. Although the words "Bereschith bara Elohim" signify "By the Verb Elohim created the heavens and the earth," it is not to be concluded that *since matter was created by the Verb* the Verb was already manifest before the creation. *Truly, it exists through all eternity*, but it manifested itself for the first time only when matter had been created. Beforehand the mysterious Infinite manifested his omnipotence and his universal goodness with the aid of the mysterious Thought, which was, albeit silent, of the same essence as the mysterious Verb. The Verb, manifested at the time of the creation of matter, existed before in the form of Thought; for if the word is able to express all that is material, it is powerless to manifest the immaterial. That is why the Scriptures say: "And Elohim said" (va yomer Elohim), *which is to say* Elohim manifested himself in the form of the Verb. *This* divine seed, through which creation came about, had just germinated, and in transforming itself from Thought into Verb it caused a noise to be heard, which noise was heard without. *The Scriptures add:* "Let there be light" (iehi or); for all light proceeds from the mystery of *the Verb.* The word "iehi" is composed of *three letters:* a Yod at the beginning and at the end and a Hé in the middle. This word is the symbol of the *heavenly* Father and Mother, designated by the letters Yod and Hé and of the *third* divine essence which proceeds from the two *former* and which is denoted by the last Yod of the word "iehi," a letter identical with the first *to show us* that all three *hypostases* are but one. *The Father,* denoted by the first Yod, is the dispenser of all the *heavenly* lights. When the materialisation of *the void* came about, by the *sound of the Verb,* denoted by the Hé, the heavenly light concealed itself, being incompatible with matter.                [Vol. I., p. 98.]

So, then, a veil exists from the very first between God and creation; creation hides God.

## 2. *The Withdrawal*

As God filled the immensity of space, there could only be room for the separated creatures if God withdrew from one part of himself. This part, freed, so to speak, from the will of God, yet

retains in a latent state the divine qualities. These
qualities, guided by Wisdom, gradually manifested
themselves and ended by giving birth to the
worlds and to all creatures and all things of which
the worlds are composed.

It is this part of God from which God has
withdrawn his direct will which forms the divine
raw material of which everything is made. All
things are, then, of the very substance of God and
yet only exist as separate beings through the
absence, the withdrawal of God.

This is the famous theory of the withdrawal,
the most characteristic of the cabalistic theories.
Wherever we come across it we shall be able with
certainty to diagnose the influence of the Cabala.

The following passage is one of the most important in the Cabala. It gives us not only the
theory of the withdrawal but also the divine person
of the Schekhina, the female power, here identified
with light, whom we shall meet again. We find
here, too, the dimmed light identified with matter.
We have already noted the rôle of this light, the
very substance of God of which the world is
made; this conception plays a rôle of the first
importance in the Cabala.

What is the "Schekhina"? "There are," says the Z.
(i., fol. 166 and 17a), "in the essence of God two lights,
one active called day, the other called night." Why these
two lights? and what is the meaning of active and passive
light? The Tiqouné Zohar, xix., replies: "When we con-

sider that the Holy One, blessed be his name, is infinite and all pervading, it can easily be understood that all idea of creation would have been impossible without the 'Zimzoum' (withdrawal). How, indeed, can water be poured into a cup already full to the brim? So the Holy One, blessed be his name, limited the holy light which constitutes his essence; not that he grew less—may God preserve us from such an opinion—God being The Whole, he can grow neither more nor less. Only, as the light of God is of such purity and brilliance that it eclipses everything, even the higher angels, even the Hayoth, even the Seraphim and Cherubim, the Holy One, blessed be his name, in order to make possible the existence of the heavenly and material worlds, withdrew his powerful light from a part of himself, as a man might bind up one of his members to keep the blood above the ligature from contact with that below. This is the way we must explain the tradition concerning the four worlds: of emanation, of creation, of formation, and of action. The first two degrees or worlds are filled with the holy light of God; all there is God, and God is all there. The two last degrees or worlds constitute that part of the essence of God in which the light has been dimmed to allow souls, angels and material worlds to subsist. It is this part of God that our holy masters designate by the name of 'Schekhina.' This is why at the beginning of Genesis there is none spoken of but Elohim, which denotes the Schekhina, because all that has been created, from the Hayoth and the Seraphim down to the smallest worm on the earth, lives in Elohim and by Elohim. It is for this same reason that our holy masters have taught us that the Schekhina has already come down six times upon earth, but not the Holy One, blessed be his name, because the creation is the work of the Schekhina and she watches over it as a mother watches over her children."     [Vol. VI., p. 346.]

We shall see that this is no metaphor, but that the Schekhina is in truth the Mother of all creatures, God being the Father.*

## 3. *Light as Substance and the Formation of Souls*

The divine light gradually thickens and forms the various souls, more and more gross the further they are from God.

But however gross they may be, they remain identical with the deity, who has only become obscured in them, and they remain, though in a diminished form, the image of God.

Note that there are three "souls" in the higher degrees; and because they are three, they are four. The first is the supreme soul, incomprehensible even to the beings on high, and therefore all the more so to those below; it is the Soul of all souls, eternally hidden and never revealed; all things are dependent on it. It is surrounded by a light as dazzling as crystal. It gives out crystalline "drops" which are united to each other as are the joints of the limbs which unite all parts of the body into one whole. It is in these drops that the supreme soul manifests itself; they form but one unity and are never separated. This supreme soul is the most hidden of all. The other soul is the female element, it is enclosed within the "drops" which constitute the strength of the first one; it is the soul of it. From these two souls united is formed (245*b*) the

*This passage, according to the texts, is sometimes attributed to the *Tiqouné Zohar* and sometimes to Louria, a sixteenth-century commentator, whose authority is considered by the cabalists to be of the very highest order.

body (that is to say the divine essence); for it is by their union the divine works are made manifest to all men, just as the body, which is the garment of the soul, makes manifest all the acts of the latter. Just as the body is united to the soul, so are united the two higher, hidden souls. The third soul is that of the righteous here below. These souls emanate from the two supreme souls, the female soul and the male soul; that is why the souls of the righteous are higher than all the celestial legions and hosts. But, we may ask, since the supreme souls are of two sides (two natures) why do the souls of the righteous descend to this world, and why are they detached from the supreme souls? The case of the souls may be compared to that of a king to whom a son was born; he sent him to a village to be brought up there until he was of age, and to receive instruction in the manners and customs to be observed in the royal palace. As soon as the King learned that his son was grown up and that his education was finished, he sent, for love of his son, the matrona, the child's mother, and to the palace she brought back the son to rejoice the heart of his father every day. In the same way, the Holy One, blessed be his name, had a son by the Matrona. And who is this son? It is the supreme, sacred soul. He sent this son to the village, that is to say this world below, so that he should grow up in it and learn the manners and customs practised in the King's palace. As soon as the King learns that his son in the village is grown up and that it is time to bring him back to the palace, he sends the Matrona to his son so that she may bring him back to the palace; for the soul does not leave this world without the Matrona coming to it and bringing it back to the King's palace, where it remains eternally.                    [Vol. II., p. 570.]

The Matrona is also the Schekhina; this passage gives us a first expression of the idea of intercourse

between the upper and the lower worlds, between
God and the soul, God and the world, the world
and man.

The following passage explains better still this
law, one of the most important in the Cabala, of
the relation between the macrocosm and the
microcosm, between God, the world and man.

Here it is as regards the world:

All that is on the earth is formed in the likeness of the
world above; and there is not the smallest object in this
world below which has not its equivalent in the world
above, which governs it. By setting in motion the objects
here below, the forces on high, which govern, are made
to act. Thus every object in this world below is the image
of a heavenly force which is set in motion by moving the
object here below. [Vol. II., p. 214.]

And as regards man:

The Holy One, blessed be his name, created man by
imprinting on him the image of the sacred kingdom,
which is the image of the Whole; it is this image which the
Holy One, blessed be his name, saw when he created the
world and all the creatures in the world (254a). This
image is the synthesis of all the spirits above and below,
undivided; it is the synthesis of all the Sephiroth, of all
their names, their epithets and their denominations.

[Vol. II., p. 598.]

This theory inclines certain commentators towards materialism, causing them to assert that
substance is identical in all its manifestations,
from that of the mineral up to God. Hence, in the

seventeenth century, the ideas of Fludd, of the
mortalists and finally of Milton himself.

When the Holy One, blessed be his name, created man,
he fashioned his body in the heavenly likeness and gave
him a sacred soul composed of three degrees as has been
said. Now the man who degrades his body ends by degrading his soul equally, seeing that the three degrees of
the soul form but one; thus by degrading "Nephesch,"
"Rouah" and "Neschama" are also degraded.

[Vol. IV., p. 155.]

## 4. *Light as Seed*

The divine light-substance is identified with
the seed of human reproduction. Hence the sanctity of the genital organs, bearers of this substance,
and the sanctity of the sexual act; ideas that we
shall see developed further on.

The young man once more began to laugh and con-
tinued speaking. As I have said, the formation of Adam
took place in the same way as the formation of the body
in a woman's womb. First came the action of the "light,"
to which corresponds the fluid of the human body, then
that of the "water," to which corresponds the "semen,"
and finally that of the firmament to which corresponds
the "coagulated semen." The face of man is formed in
the womb of woman. But as Adam did not issue from the
womb of a woman, his face was formed by a single operation of the three elements above. Thus in the beginning
man did not have the form he now has; there was no
difference between a male and a female body. It was only
when Adam lay with Eve that their mutual desire imprinted on their bodies the present forms which dis·

tinguish the male and the female. That is why the Scriptures said: "And he created in his own image and in his own likeness." It was no longer in the image or likeness of God, but in the image of a body in which the male is distinguished from the female. That is why the Scriptures say: "And Adam knew Eve his wife, who conceived and bare Cain." The body she had in her womb began to take the form of an ape (after the fall). But after the birth of Abel, the devil, who strove to dishonour the body more and more, lost power (768*a*). The body was then, for the most part, cleansed of its impurity. Thus Seth already had the form of the men of these days. [Vol. IV., p. 115.]

The Scriptures say: "And God said: Let there be light and there was light." It would have sufficed to say: "And it was so." Why this repetition? In order to show us that light will once more shine on the world at the end of time. The primitive light is divided into five degrees; and that is why in the chapter on creation the word "light" is found five times. This light appears in three different forms. Now it appears actually as light, now in the form of water, and now in that of firmament; that is why the words "water" and "firmament" are also repeated five times in the chapter on the Creation. It is by reason of these three forms of primitive Light that man is made in the image of God: children are wont to resemble the father, and that by reason of "the light," that is to say the fluid which runs through all the members of the body and produces "semen"; the "water," that is to say the liquid "semen" (176*b*); and the firmament, that is to say the coagulated "semen"; for the formation of the body only becomes perceptible when the "semen" thickens. Primitive Light having the three forms of " light," "water " and "firmament" and man being formed of (through) primitive Light, it follows that man must necessarily have

89

the image of God. If man were composed only of the pure elements, used in the formation of Adam, he would be less disposed to sin. But it is the turbid waters, coming to mingle in the formation of bodies, which give the devil a hold over man. It is this power of the devil over the body which causes the death of children. That is why the word "meoroth" is written without Vav. [Vol. IV., p. 114.]

The "head of the righteous one" denotes the sign of the Covenant; for just as the head of a jar is found where the opening for the pouring of the liquid it contains has been made, so is designated by the name of "head of the righteous one" that organ qui semen injicit feminae; for the man who keeps in all its purity the sign of the Covenant and who observes the commandments of the Law is called Righteous from his head to his feet. It is the sign of the Covenant which contains all the blessings of the world; and when the blessings of the world above come down here below, they rest on the head of the Righteous as has just been said. [Vol. II., p. 235.]

## 5. *The Responsibility of all Beings*

Man holding the highest rank in the lower worlds, his fall involved that of the other creatures; one finds in the *Zohar* the germ of the idea of the kinship of men and animals. This idea is strengthened by the theories of reincarnation that we shall study later on. The conception of the joint responsibility of nature and of *animals* with man in his fall becomes one of the proofs of their similarity of constitution and essence. These ideas are, moreover, in harmony with that of the divine matter common to all beings. Thus the conceptions of the materialists and evolutionists will harmonise with some cabalistic theories.

As soon as Adam stood up all creatures saw him, feared him and followed him as servitors follow their king: all in the world did as he did. So he said: "Come, let us adore him; let us cast ourselves down and bless the Lord God who created us." And when Adam prostrated himself before the "other side" and clave to it, all creatures followed his example. That is why Adam caused the death of all in the world. From that moment man became susceptible to changes; sometimes he is good, sometimes he is bad; sometimes he is alive, sometimes he is dead, because nature itself having followed Adam's example, became subject to changes, when God had willed that man should always remain stable.     [Vol. II., p. 471.]

One rather obscure passage is worth quoting, the note of the commentators Pauly and Lafuma recording a cabalistic tradition that we shall meet again. Man, but for his fall, would have enjoyed earthly immortality. This idea is also to be found in Saint Augustine. But certain cabalists draw from it the conclusion that when the chosen escape the effects of the fall they may attain immortality in their human form upon earth.

The Scriptures say: "Unto Adam also and to his wife did the Lord God make coats of skins and clothed them." Did Adam and his wife have no skins before the sin? But the truth is that the word "skins" denotes glorious raiment after the sin. Rabbi Hyia put forward the objection: "Were they worthy of glorious raiment after the sin?" Rabbi

Eleazar answered him: "The skins themselves were glorious raiment before the sin and this raiment became rough skins only after the sin."* [Vol. VI., p. 11.]


## 6. *The Forbidden Mysteries*

One of the most frequently emphasised consequences of these ideas is the injunction given to man not to try to understand God and his mysteries: a vain and sacrilegious undertaking since God is the unfathomable.

Let us end this section by quoting two of these passages which forbid man to aspire to too much knowledge. To seek to know too much is to risk offending the deity, and, moreover, there are secrets the very possession of which is dangerous. It is for man's good that God at times forbids him knowledge.

Eternal wisdom can belong only to God, man being too weak to possess it. It is because the Holy One, blessed be his name, had caused the mystery of Wisdom to come down into the world, that men became corrupted to such a degree that they wished to declare war on him. Therefore, God had concealed from the first man the mystery of higher wisdom; and it was through this mystery being revealed to him (76a) that Adam knew the heavenly degrees; and he ended by cleaving to the arch tempter, thereby causing the fount of Wisdom to dry up within

* That is to say, without sin, man would have arrived at the state of glory without passing through death. But sins made the skins rough, and this forced him to pass through corruption and death before reaching the state of glory.

him. After he had done penance, the mystery which had
been revealed to him, and which he had forgotten after
his sin, was once more revealed to him, but not in the
same measure as before. The heavenly book containing
the mystery of Wisdom was passed on by Adam to other
men, who, in their turn, having fathomed the mystery,
angered God. [Vol. I., p. 446.]

When he was come to Haran, Abraham began to study
the causes of the superiority of the centre of the earth
over the rest of the world; *for, on approaching Palestine,
Abraham had felt its beneficent influence.* Not being able
to succeed in this, Abraham began to count and make
very abstruse calculations about the heavenly rulers who
govern the different parts of the world; and aided by his
knowledge of the courses and influence of the stars, he
came to know the importance, size and influence of each
of the heavenly bodies; and he came equally to know,
with the aid of his learning, the hierarchy of the divers
heavenly powers which rule over the countless worlds.
But all his efforts remained fruitless each time he sought
to penetrate the essence and importance of the supreme
Power on which all others depend. Seeing all the efforts
put forth by Abraham, in his desire for knowledge, the
Holy One, blessed be his name, appeared to him and
said: "Lekh Lekha," *which means:* look into thy heart,
know thyself and seek to amend thy ways; but "leave
thy country," *which means:* abandon these studies on the
moral influences of countries; and "leave thy kindred,"
*which means:* cast off this knowledge which consists of
foretelling the future of men by the stars, and which
asserts that the day, the hour and the minute of the birth
of every man exercise an influence on his future.
[Vol. I., p. 458.]

## [B] THE SEXUAL LAW

*1. God male and female. Sexual life within the deity. 2. The Matrona or Schekhina, an intermediary power and a mediator with God. 3. Man in the image of God : hermaphrodite at first, then unisexual. 4. The twin souls. 5. The cosmic rôle of the sexual union. 6. The conception of woman : reason and passion.*

## 1. *God Male and Female. Sexual Life within the Deity*

The starting point of these conceptions is evidently in primitive beliefs: the only authentic case of creation that we know is the birth of the child; consequently the creation of the world and the birth of all creatures must be accomplished in the same way, by the union of male and female. This necessitates two powers, two gods. Often the Sun is the male and the Earth the female: as in Spenser. Sometimes the Sun is identified with God: as in Fludd and the English mortalists of the seventeenth century.

In this first passage, the simplest, the most "primitive" that I have found, it is God and the Earth who unite in the sexual act.

Now, a tradition teaches us that the word "created," "Behibaram" ought to be read as two separate words, behi baram; which signifies that God created (the heavens and the earth) by the Hé. And he who is on high is the father of all; he it is who created everything, who fecundated the earth which grew big and brought forth "fruits" (tholdoth). It was fecundated as a female is

94

fecundated by a male. Rabbi Eleazar says "All things were latent in the earth from the time it was created; but *it* did not manifest them in its fruits until the sixth day of creation. . . ." [Vol. I., p. 268.]

But this primitive stage could not satisfy the metaphysicians of the Cabala. There is only one God. Therefore it can only be within the deity that the sexual act takes place.

The feminine Power emanated from God, is his daughter. That introduces the theme of sacred incest, Father-Daughter, which results in the creation.

Here is the theory explained by the symbol of letters:

When the Supreme Thought experienced a mysterious joy, a luminous ray escaped from the Thought and drew the forty-two letters together, and it was this union which resulted in the birth of the world above and of the one below. This is the mystery which God makes known to those who fear him. The letter Beth with which the Scriptures begin is the female Element; the letter Aleph is the male Element. The Scriptures say: "Bereschith bara Elohim," which means that in the beginning Elohim created the letter Beth, the female Element. The union of Aleph with Beth resulted in the birth of all the other letters; and the union of the Yod with the Hé, male and female Elements, resulted in the birth of the Vav.

[Vol. IV., p. 256.]

But the sexes are relative things in the *Zohar*. We shall see further on the changes of sex that become necessary. Let it be stated first of all that a being may be male in relation to another being and female in relation to a third. After sacred incest, we come to sacred inversion.

When the Scriptures speak of the "King" without any other specification, they denote that King which, although supreme, forms the female Element in relation to the supreme "Point," the most mysterious of all. And although this King is the female Element when compared to the supreme "Point," which constitutes the male Element, he is male when compared to the King below.

[Vol. III., p. 14.]

From the sexual union issues the world: the culminating point of the creation is the union of the two divine powers.

The Scriptures add: "And the evening and the morning *together formed* the sixth day." Why do not the Scriptures use the Hé *as a determinate prefix* for all the other days of the Creation, *as for* the sixth day which is designated by the word "ha-schischi" (the sixth)? Because, when the creation of the world was finished, the male became united with the female in the union of the Hé to form a whole. That is also why the Scriptures add: "The heavens and the earth were finished and all the host of them," which means: they have formed of all things a complete and harmonious unity.     [Vol. I., p. 273.]

This divine sexual union continues and upholds the world. It is the idea of continuous creation, expressed in this cabalistic and primitive scheme.

The male generating organ is at the extremity of the body and symbolises the Sephira "Yesod." This has access to the female region called Sion, a mysterious and hidden region, as it is written: "The Eternal has chosen Sion and has desired it for his residence." On the eve of the Sabbath, when the Matrona lies with the King, they form but one body. The Holy One, blessed be his name, seats himself on his throne; all things are perfect, and all things receive the name of the Holy One, that they may be blessed through all eternity. I have deferred the manifestation of these words until this day, which shall remain crowned by them for the world to come. Happy is my lot! When the Matrona is united to the King, all the worlds are blessed and every universe is full of joy. [Vol. VI., p. 118.]

Those who understand this mystery know how to participate in it. Note here the first connection between human sexual union and divine sexual union. We shall see its importance later.

This confirms the remark of Rabbi Eleazar, according to which the Scriptures use the term "sixth day" to denote Friday, which is done for no other day of the week, so as to show us that on that day the union of the King and the Matrona takes place; for it is in the night of Friday that the Matrona is united to the King and takes her delight in him. It is for this reason that on Friday the Israelites gathered two lots of manna, one for the King and the other for the Matrona. It is for this reason also that man must place the loaf on the table on the night of Friday, which is the beginning of the Sabbath, in order to draw down the blessing from above, for the blessing is not shed on an unspread table. The doctors who understand the mystery of the union of the King with the Matrona on the night of Friday keep their conjugal relations for the night of Friday. The Sabbath day is the synthesis of all the days of the week. [Vol. III., p. 279.]

The benefits of the divine union overflow over all the lower worlds; and the lower worlds collaborate in this union:

The seventh palace is devoid of all form; it constitutes the Mystery of mysteries, before which is hung the veil which separates it from all the other palaces, so that no man may see the two "cherubim" who are behind this veil. That is why this palace is called the "Holy of Holies," because it alone sees the Spirit of spirits, the Spirit which animates all the others and sheds light on them. It is at the moment when all the spirits unite with the supreme Spirit that all the lights of the palace overflow from the Holy of Holies and flood all the worlds. All light which comes down below may be compared to the seed that the male imparts to the female. Now the perfect union cannot be accomplished unless the seed be imparted through the seventh palace above to the seventh palace below; it is then only that the union will be perfect (45b), as it should be. Happy is the lot of the man who knows how to bring about this union. [Vol. I., p. 263.]

In this state of things, if one recalls that the total God is completely inaccessible, the secondary feminine power, Schekhina or Matrona, necessarily becomes the intermediary power between God and his creatures.

## 2. *The Matrona or Schekhina, an Intermediary Power and a Mediator with God*

God, unknowable and inaccessible, has entrusted his powers to the Matrona. He is above any action which would enable man to know him. The

Schekhina is therefore the part of God which is revealed. She is the mother of all creatures, who are made of her substance. Through affection for her children, she will be their mediator with the inaccessible Father.

We shall find her in this rôle when we turn our attention to the Justice of God.

The word "Israel" denotes Israel above, and the "Angel of God" denotes God himself, for thus it is written: "And the Lord God walked before them." Is it compatible with the glory of a king to allow his matrona to make war alone and let her be the mediator? But the king may be compared to a king who wedded a matrona of great merit. When the king learned to appreciate the high qualities of his matrona, which surpassed those of all other matronas, he wondered how he could reward so much virtue. Then said the king to himself: The whole world must learn of the high qualities of my matrona so that she may be the absolute mistress of my house. Accordingly the king sent out a proclamation, worded in the following way: All the powers of the king are entrusted to the matrona. Further, the king entrusted to the matrona all his arms, he made all the captains of his hosts subordinate to her, and delivered unto her all the gems and all the royal treasures. The king added: From this day on, no man can have speech with me without first presenting himself to the matrona. In the same way, the Holy One, blessed be his name, through his great love for the "Community of Israel," entrusted all his power to the Matrona. The King said: "There are sixty queens, and eighty women of the second rank, and countless maidens; but one alone is my dove, and my well-beloved, she stands alone, etc. My whole house is in her hands." The King issued a proclamation worded thus: All the powers of the King are entrusted to the Matrona. The King delivered unto her, moreover, his arms, lances, swords, bows, arrows, daggers, and slings, and made subordinate to her all the captains of the heavenly hosts. That is why the Scriptures say: "Here is the bed of Solomon, surrounded by sixty men among the most valiant of the strongest of Israel, all bearing swords and all very experienced in war." The King said to his Matrona: From this day on, the conduct of my wars is given unto thee, my armies as well as the captains of the heavenly hosts are in thy hands. From this day on, it is thou who shalt watch over me, for thus it is written ... "The one who watches over Israel." From this day on, whosoever has need of me may speak with me only through the Matrona, for thus it is written: Let not Aaron go into the Sanctuary except through This (Zoth). Thus, the Matrona is the perfect Mediator with the King, and all powers are in her hands, and this is what makes the glory of the Matrona. [Vol. III., p. 231.]

Mankind has its part to play in the union of God and the Matrona.

The old Hindu conception, to which we shall come back later, is that the deity divided himself into fragments and that these fragments are the various creatures. The purpose of the sacrifice is the reconstitution of this first deity, and the sacrifice is, therefore, the ultimate purpose of the world's existence as well as its basis.

A similar conception is to be found in the Cabala. The mission of the sacrificer is to bring about the divine union. But here this notion is translated into the sexual plane.

We shall see that the Cabala did not consider, as did the Hindus, that the sacrifice was enough in itself, and added to it the example, the instigation of human sexual union, a still more primitive conception to be met with again presently. Here we have the sacrifice reconstituting the divine sexual unity.

Note that the mission of the Priests and Levites was to unite the left side and the right side. Rabbi Hizqiya says: Although it comes to the same thing, I have heard this explanation expounded in another way. The mission of the Priests is to awaken the left side, that of the Levites to awaken the right side, to bring about thus the union of the male and female elements, as it is written: "He puts his left hand under my head and he clasps me with his right hand." When desire unites the male element to the female element, the worlds are blessed and joy reigns above and below. Thus the mission of the Priests and Levites is to bring about by sacrifices the desire of the left side for the right side; a desire which constitutes the basis of the world and the joy of all creatures both above and below. [Vol. II., p. 565.]

The sacrifice celebrated by men is an aphrodisiac for the deity.

3. *Man in the Image of God: Hermaphrodite at first, then Unisexual*

We see once more in operation the fundamental law of the Cabala, the law of correlation: the worlds below are constructed on the model of the worlds above. Nay, more, they are the worlds above less well perceived, but essentially the deity himself. This has a two-fold result; first of all, by this is explained the creation: man has two sexes because there are two sexes in God; then, to man is given a rôle of first importance: as he is God, when he is united to woman, God is united to the Matrona.

Here is primitive man, the human hermaphrodite:

The Scriptures say, moreover: "And Elohim said: Let us make man in our image." They do not say: "Let us make the man," but "Let us make man," so as to exclude the "Man" above, who is formed of the complete name. When the Man above is complete, the man below is equally so. Jehovah is the male side, and Elohim is the female side. Thus to make man in the image of God, he had to be made both male and female. Yod denotes the male, Hé the female; Vav issues from both. That is why the Scriptures say: "Male and female created he them; he blessed them and gave them the name of man (Adam)," that is to say, he gave them the name of the "man" seated on the heavenly throne, whose form they had received, as it is written: "And above the throne could be seen something which appeared like unto a man."

[Vol. IV., p. 142.]

God divided this man into two: a male and a female.

And tradition teaches us also that Adam had been created with two faces; therefore he was not alone! He could not find a helpmeet in her, seeing that she was in his ribs and was joined to the back of him. Adam was

therefore alone. "I will make him an helpmeet for him."
What does "for him" mean? I will that he be united to
his wife face to face. God cut him open, separating the
female from him, as it is written: "And he took one of his
ribs (ahath)." "Ahath" denotes the female. " . . . And
he brought her unto Adam." And he decked her as a
bride and led her to Adam so that she might lie with him.
When they formed two, they received the serene blessings.                                    [Vol. V., p. 123.]

This primitive state of man, undivided into
sexes, was a very imperfect state. We shall see
that there has been no lack of speculation on this
point. Here we have first of all the assertion that
the creation remained incomplete as long as the
normal sexual union had not taken place, and the
assertion of the influence of the lower grades of
being on the higher ones. This is, perhaps, one
of the reasons for the creation. God could only
attain to his own union with the Matrona if man
first of all accomplished a similar union. The
lower beings had to be created so that the deity
might attain to the full enjoyment of his own
sexual life.

Note that Adam and Eve were in the beginning created
joined the one to the side of the other. Why were they
not created joined face to face? By reason of the words of
the Scriptures: ". . . For the Lord God had not yet
caused it to rain upon the earth." The union of man, a
being higher than all the other works of creation, the
union of man, we say, with his wife, had to be modelled
upon nature. Therefore it is only when the union of

heaven and earth took place for the first time, a union which was made manifest by the rain, that man was united face to face with his wife. How do we know that *the acts of the higher ones are modelled on those of the lower ones?* We know it from the Tabernacle, for thus it is written: "And the Tabernacle was set up." *Now we know through a tradition that these words of the Scriptures denote the Heavenly Tabernacle.* Thus the Heavenly Tabernacle was set up only after that of the earth. It was the same with the face to face union of man and his wife before God caused rain to fall upon the earth. That is why the Scriptures say: "And there was not a man." The Scriptures understand by that, that as long as Eve was not yet created, man was an unfinished being; man only became complete after the creation of Eve. This mystery is already indicated to us by the fact that in the whole passage relating to the creation of woman the letter "Samekh," *which means* "support," "help," "succour," does not appear, although the teachers have said that the word "Ezer" (help) means that the woman was created to serve as a helper to the man, she became a "helpmeet" only from the time that the union was made face to face. Such is the meaning of the words of the Scriptures: "They are united the one to the other for all eternity; they are made according to truth and equity." By that word "united" the Scriptures denote the male and female whose union in this lower world will continue in the higher world for all eternity. The Scriptures say: "For the Lord God had not yet caused rain to fall upon the earth." The Scriptures mean that the perfect union of the man and the woman did not yet exist because this union was not yet manifest in nature. And this perfect union consists of a holy union face to face. Therefore the Scriptures add immediately afterwards: "And there went up a mist from the earth and watered the whole face of the ground." That is the desire felt by the female for the male: mists rise first of all from the earth to the heavens; and after forming clouds, the heavens water the earth. Notice that it is the same with the works of man.                    [Vol. I., p. 216.]

This line of cogitation leads to pantheism of a kind: all souls are one with the supreme soul. But we can find also in the following text that the ideas on sex can be a starting point for the ideas on God's Wrath and the failure of the earlier attempts at creation.

In his formation as male and female man resembles Jehovah Elohim, that is the Ancient of Days and "the Lesser Face." The Scriptures say that he formed men of the dust of the ground, which means that he formed one image inside the other. The Scriptures add: "And he breathed into his nostrils the breath of life." This is the seal imprinted on a man to enable him to rise to the most sublime mystery, to fathom the depth of all that is hidden; for the souls of all who live above and below are dependent on the soul of souls, in whom they have their existence. And he who lifts up his soul to God can attain by successive stages to the highest stage of all. As all souls form but one unity with the soul of souls, it follows that he who loses his soul causes a break in continuity. Therefore he and all remembrance of him are exterminated from this world for all eternity.          [Vol. V., p. 366.]

(142a) We learned in the Occult Book "membrum virile divisum est partes in duas quarum unam 'Hésed' appelant, aliam injicimus in pudenda mulieris. Habet quandam imaginem litterae Yod in fine ubi semen ejicit." A tradition teaches us, moreover, that as long as the ornaments of the King were not complete the Ancient of Ancients built worlds which did not last; and the "Female" element of Wrath was only appeased when "Grace" descended from on high. Then was Wrath appeased. Now the fecundation of the female takes place "cum fine virilis membri. Homines autem terrarum anteriorum non usi sunt coitu," as it is written: "Such are the kings which reigned in the land of Edom, before the children of Israel had a king."

### 4. *The Twin Souls*

Man, the soul, is created an hermaphrodite. He is divided into twin souls, one male, the other female, which must meet one another and unite.

The cabalists considered that this search is difficult. There are many obstacles in the way. For instance, if a man remains chaste in his youth, he has the right to ask God to give him in marriage any woman who pleases him. God is obliged to bring about this union, even if the woman is the twin soul of another man. Yet God is equally obliged to bring about in the end the union of the predestined couple. That is to say, God having first of all satisfied the chaste man, by giving him the woman of his desire, is forced to get rid of him so that the woman can be united to her twin-soul spouse.

This explanation was probably thought out to justify the marriage of David and Bathsheba. The latter was the twin soul of David, but Uriah, a chaste man, having asked God for her, had obtained her. It was therefore necessary that Uriah should die, and the action of David in having him killed was inspired by the Holy One (blessed be his name, unfailingly adds the *Zohar*, with an utter lack of humour).

This is only one of the difficulties that the Holy One has to overcome in order to bring about the necessary marriages. Let us see him at work:

Note that all the souls in this world, which constitute the fruit of the works of the Holy One, blessed be his name, form, before their descent to earth, but one unity, all being part of one and the same mystery. And when they descend to this world below, they separate into males and females; and males and females unite. Note, furthermore, that the female's desire for the male produces a vital spirit, and that the male's desire for the female also produces a spirit. Now, as the desire of the body arouses also the desire of the soul, it follows that the birth of a male and female must necessarily cause the descent of a male soul and a female soul which are united together. It is only after their descent to this world that they separate and *go to animate* two *different bodies, that of a man and that of a woman.* And it is the Holy One, blessed be his name, who unites them again later, *when they marry.* The responsibility for the unions of men and women is entrusted to no heavenly ruler; it is the Holy One himself, blessed be his name, who brings them about; for he alone knows how to accomplish them in a fitting manner. Happy is the lot of the man who lives a decent life and walks in the way of truth; for he unites one soul with another, just as they were before their descent to earth, seeing that it is only when man walks in the right path that he is a perfect man.          [Vol. I., p. 493.]

Here we see the difficulty of accomplishing these unions strongly emphasised.

Note that when the union of the Husband and Wife takes place, (208*a*) all the souls leave the celestial river above which represents "fate." These souls descend pell-mell below, male and female souls together. When the time for marriage comes, the souls must find each other again, each male soul must find the female soul which was his mate before the descent to earth. That is why tradition says that the making of marriages constitutes as hard a task as the separation of the waters of the Red Sea. To divide the sea, it was necessary to divide the heavenly region corresponding to that of the Red Sea into as many paths as there were passages in the sea for the crossing of the Israelites. To enable an event to happen here below, a similar event must take place above, everything here below being but the reflection of the world above.

[Vol. II., p. 432.]

Yet man does not really exist, does not enter into communion with the Schekhina until the true union is accomplished.

And when does the Schekhina definitely take up her abode with man? When the latter marries, "et quum signum foederis suum in locum ponit." For a tradition tells us that the letters Vav and Hé are for this reason placed in alphabetical order next to each other, because the Vav is the symbol of the male element, while the Hé is the symbol of the female element. These two elements are united. So when the husband and wife are united both form but one, and a beam of heavenly grace covers them. This beam emanates from the side of the male element. It is called "hesed" (grace), according to the words of the Scriptures: "The Grace of God (hésed El) is everlasting." For this beam issues from the supreme wisdom and penetrates the male element, which imparts it to the female element.      [Vol. I., pp. 536-537.]

The harmony between the human male and female on the one hand and the divine male and female on the other is still more emphasised in the following passage which introduces another theory: that of the necessary inferiority of woman. As the Schekhina proceeds from God and is inferior to God, woman proceeds from man and is inferior to him. But she is also necessary to him and consequently holy and powerful.

And when they are united they appear absolutely as one body. From that we deduce that a man alone is considered as a half-body. All is peace when they are united, all truly appears to be one body. And, in truth, it is so. Here also, when the male is united to the female, both constitute one single body, and all worlds rejoice, for all receive the blessing of this perfect body. And this is the mystery of the verse: "The Lord God blessed the seventh day and hallowed it." All things were perfect in one single body, for the Matrona was united to the King, forming but one body. Hence that day is the day of blessings. That is why whosoever is neither male nor female (who is not married) is called a "half-body"; a blessing cannot be bestowed on a thing which is faulty or imperfect; it can only be bestowed on a perfect region and on a complete object. Incomplete things can neither exist nor receive blessings eternally. The beauty of Woman proceeds wholly from the beauty of Man. We have expounded these things and they are known to the disciples.

To the female element are attached all creatures here below. From her they draw their nourishment and their knowledge. Just as the Mother is united to the body (of the King) and the whole body is fed by her, so is she united to, and so does she feed, those below. It is written: "Say unto Wisdom, thou art my sister." There are two wisdoms: that of the female element is called "Little Wisdom" when compared to the other. That is why the Scriptures say: "We have a little sister and she has no breasts. She is small when in exile, but she is big and powerful since she is the complement with whom the King associates himself. . . ."                    [Vol. VI., p. 117.]

Here is an example of cabalistic interpretations: a very simple Bible phrase gives rise to what follows. To the rabbis of the *Zohar* all things are in every thing. Any idea can be extracted from any text.

Knowing himself to be guilty, Hezekiah began by turning his face to the wall, which means towards the Schekhina against whom he had sinned; for the mystery of the Schekhina envelops all women; and that is why the Schekhina abides only with him who is united to a woman.                    [Vol. II., p. 501.]

## 5. *The Cosmic Rôle of the Sexual Union*

The human sexual union is the fulfilment of the divine sexual union: a conclusion drawn from the pantheism latent in the Cabala, and also from the primitive conceptions which are at the very root of these speculations. Evidence has often been collected proving that savages frequently indulge in sexual relations in order to stir up the divine powers to do the same, and, in doing so, to beget and produce creatures and things which are useful. Abundant harvests are sometimes ensured in this way, Earth allowing herself to be fecundated by God, who is, at times, the Sun. I will quote, later, some well-known passages of Frazer on this point.

The Cabala raises these ideas to a higher intellectual level. God created the world because he was both male and female, and did so by uniting these two parts. It is in this state of complete union with himself that he is the creative Power. Man being a part of the divine substance, the same phenomenon occurs in him. It is only while sexual relations are taking place that man is a complete being. Then it is that he is in full co-partnership with the deity, then it is that he is himself a creator.

But God, by the withdrawal, freed the souls from his direct dominion. In order that God's own union with the Matrona may be brought about, the freed beings of opposite sexes must also unite. Otherwise, within God, who is the whole, comprising even those freed parts of himself, there would remain a certain region in which this union would not be accomplished. Man must therefore indulge in sexual relations, so that God may unite with the Matrona. Doubtless, had it not been for the withdrawal, the Matrona would have remained non-manifest, latent only within God. To bring about this union, God had, therefore, first of all to withdraw, and then induce the freed men to indulge in sexual relations.

Note that each day a heavenly voice cries unto men: This union depends on you alone. Such is the meaning of the words (200*b*): "Take for yourselves the firstfruits of the Lord God." But, we may ask, how can a man bring about this union? The Scriptures reply: "Every man will offer it right willingly." This means: it suffices that a man should fear his Master, pray devoutly and have an upright heart for the bride to adorn herself to appear before her bridegroom accompanied by her virgins. All those who accompany her are likewise adorned. At the ritual, "It is meet and right," the Matrona and her virgins begin to adorn themselves. And at the ritual, "Who delivereth Israel . . ." the sacred King goes to meet the Matrona and receive her. He clasps her with his right arm, and then throws his left arm round the Matrona's neck; and both unite in a kiss. Therefore we must recite the three first blessings of the prayer devoutly and reverently. At the moment when the King is united to the Matrona in a kiss, we should make known our wishes, for the moment is propitious. After man has made all his requests to the King and the Matrona in the first three blessings of the prayer, he communes with himself a while in order to recite the three other blessings. I have heard this thing from the "Holy Lamp," and he has authorised me to reveal it unto men like yourselves, full of faith and zeal. If man participates body and soul in the union of the King and the Matrona, the Holy One, blessed be his name, names it "peace"; and when such a man dies, his soul rises and passes through all the heavens without let or hindrance; to this soul (201*a*) are opened the thirteen treasures of delightful perfumes without any one saying him nay. [Vol. IV., pp. 201-202.]

These speculations are dangerous. For they seem to show, to a certain extent, that the life of God is dependent on man. During the eighteenth century in England, for instance, these conceptions mark a phase of transition towards unbelief, towards the idea that man created God, that the very centre of the deity is in man and not in God. And this comes fairly near to doing away with the idea of God altogether.

Of course, nothing in the *Zohar* tends in this direction, which leads essentially to the out-and-out scepticism of the West. To true cabalists this mystery is sacred and divine:

(66*b*) *It is written:* "I will make my covenant with thee." Rabbi Eleazar says: "We infer from this verse that the making of the Covenant on high conforms to the making of the Covenant below, and that is why the Scriptures say: 'I will make my covenant with thee.'" Rabbi Eleazar says, moreover: "We conclude from this verse that when men in this world below are righteous, they make the Covenant on high as well as below." Rabbi Simeon says: "A word *has been said on this subject*, which holds a hidden meaning. *This is what has been said:* The desire of the male for the female is only aroused after a transport of jealousy. Note that this saying holds the following mystery: When there is a righteous man in this world below, the Schekhina abides with him and never leaves him again. Then it is that the desire of Him on high is enflamed with love for the Schekhina, like to the desire felt by the male for the female when he is moved by jealousy. That is why the Scriptures say: 'I will make my covenant with thee.' *These words signify*: 'Because of you, I feel desire for the Schekhina.'"

[Vol. I., p. 391.]

And here is the metaphorical transposition: the love-union of God and of the community of the righteous.

Although the hours which precede midnight are also part of the night, the Holy One, blessed be his name, does not descend until midnight into the Garden of Eden, there to take his pleasure with the Righteous. For this reason man must devote this hour to the study of the Law. Even as all the Righteous, assembled in the Garden of Eden, listen at this hour to the voice of the man, as it is written: "O thou, that dost dwell in the gardens, the friends are ready to listen; let me hear thy voice." "The one" who "dwells in the gardens" denotes the "Community of Israel," who praise the Holy One, blessed be his name, during the night. Happy is the lot of him who, associating himself with the "Community of Israel," praises God at this hour. At the dawn of day, the Holy One, blessed be his name, takes his pleasure with the "Community of Israel," holding out to it the staff of mercy, for thus it is written: "The Lord God sends forth his mercy during the day, and at night I sing unto him a song." This mercy is not vouchsafed only to the "Community of Israel" but to all those associated with it. That is the reason for the name "roe of the morning." Rabbi Simeon says: Before dawn the sky grows dark, and the darkness deepens in intensity, that is the hour in which the wife is united to the husband, even as tradition teaches

us that at this hour the wife is in the arms of her husband. When the sun rises it drives away all shadows. But during the night all doors are closed, asses bray and dogs bark. After midnight the King arises, and the Matrona begins to sing. The King then knocks at the door of the palace saying: "Open unto me, my well-beloved sister," etc.
[Vol. III., p. 210.]

Here is the metaphysical explanation, by impulsion from below.

Note that the world above is set in motion by impulsion from the one below, and the world below is set in motion by the one above. Smoke which rises from here below lights the lamps above, so that all the lights shine in the sky; and thus it is that all the worlds are blessed. As it rises, the smoke from here below delights the sacred shapes above, who are set over this world; and it is this pleasure which inspires them with desire for the ranks above them, for thus it is written: "The lion cubs roar after their prey," etc. Thus the sacred beings on high feel a desire to unite with the sacred beings above them, and so on, until the King is united to the Matrona; and it is thus that, through desire below, the waters here below gush forth first of all to receive the waters from above; for the seed above does not gush forth without a previous desire below. [Vol. II., p. 565.]

But the *Zohar* does not lose sight of the fact that the aim of sexual union is creation. Through it, in God, the world was created, then man: from it spring the souls of the righteous.

It is the Hé, which, filled with light from above (60*b*), also makes the souls of the righteous here below spring forth, as we have already said. According to another interpretation, *the words* "Drink of the water of thy fount" denote King David, who was made to say by the Scriptures: "Who (mi) will give me water from the fount which is at Bethlehem?" *The word* "stream" denotes Abraham. *The word* "of" (mithokh) denotes Jacob, who is the figure in between. *Finally, the word* "Thy fount" denotes Isaac who is called "the fount of living water."

In this verse is expressed the sacred and sublime mystery of the patriarchs to whom David belongs. The desire of the female for the male is aroused only when the female spirit enters her; then only does the female send forth her waters towards the fecundating substance of the male above. In the same way, the Synod of Israel experiences desire for the Holy One, blessed be his name, only because it is filled with the spirit of the righteous; it is then only that the Synod of Israel sends forth its waters towards the fecundating substance of the male; then passion becomes equal, *that is to say, common to male and female*, so that the male and female are bound together as one. All delight in this state; it is denoted by the term: "The Holy One, blessed be his name, walks about and takes his pleasure in company with the souls of the righteous."

[Vol. I., p. 353.]

*It is written:* "Male and female created he them." Rabbi Simeon says: *These two verses at the beginning of the fifth chapter of Genesis* contain great mysteries. In the words, "Male and female created he them," is expressed the supreme mystery which constitutes the glory of God, who is inaccessible to human intelligence and is the object of the Faith. It was through this mystery that man was created. Note that man was created through the same mystery as heaven and earth; for, for the creation of heaven and earth, the Scriptures use the term: "This is

the genesis of heaven and earth"; and for the creation of
man they employ a similar term: "Here is the book of
the genesis of man." Moreover, for the creation of heaven
and earth, the Scriptures use the term: "be hibaram"
(when they were created); and for the creation of man
the Scriptures use an analogous term: "be iom hiba ram"
(in the day they were created). The Scriptures say: "Male
and female created he them." We infer from this that
every shape which does not represent the male and the
female does not resemble the heavenly shape. This mystery has already been explained. Note that the Holy One,
blessed be his name, does not make his abode where the
male and female are not united; he showers his blessings
only there where the male and female are united. That is
why the Scriptures say: "He blessed them and called
their name Adam." Thus the Scriptures do not say, "He
blessed him and called his name Adam," because God
only blesses when the male and female are united. The
male alone does not deserve even the name of man, as
long as he is not united to the female; that is why the
Scriptures say: "And he gave them the name of man."
[Vol. I., p. 320.]

And the *Zohar* calls down curses on the head of
those who do not assist the divine work by procreating.

*It is written:* "And the Lord God blessed them and
said: Be fruitful and multiply," etc. This is the commandment to be assiduous in this world in the procreation
and begetting of children to spread the glory of the sacred
name in all directions by producing spirits and souls for
the glorification of the Holy One, blessed be his name,
above and below. Whosoever is not assiduous in keeping
the commandment to procreate diminishes the Shape of

his Master and prevents him from descending here below. The lack of new souls descending here below prevents the Schekhina from coming down to this earth, since it is the souls who constitute the glory of the King in this world, for thus it is written: "The multitude of the people is the glory of the King and the small number of the subjects is the shame of the prince." The King is allured to this world by the number of souls; and if the number of souls in this world is lessened, the Shape of the King is diminished (273). The man who abstains from procreating is as guilty as if he shed the blood of his neighbour; for he prevents a reproduction of the heavenly Shape since man is made in the image of God. It is for this reason that it is right that man should be assiduous in keeping the commandment to procreate, so that the glory of God may be spread in all directions.          [Vol. II., p. 641.]

## 6. *The Conception of Woman : Reason and Passion*

From these ideas arises a special conception of the rôle and place of woman. She is the Matrona on earth. She is, therefore, in subjection to the husband as the Matrona is to God, but she is also the glory of the husband as the Matrona is the glory of God. She has her dignity and her rights and is in no way a slave.

Her special domain is the direction of the house.

In sexual matters she must be treated with respect, and not as an instrument of pleasure. Her consent must be obtained, and through affection.

. . . until that time, it is the father and mother who have charge of their daughter; but as soon as she is united

to her husband the latter must come and abide with her;
for the house is hers, and he must consult her *about all
things which concern* the affairs of the house. That is
why the Scriptures say: "And having come to a certain
place, he passed the night there, for the sun had already
set."

The Scriptures mean that Jacob obtained permission.
We infer from this that whoever is united to his wife must
first of all obtain her consent by means of loving and
tender words; if he does not obtain this consent, he must
go no further; for the union of man and wife must be
voluntary and without coercion.        [Vol. I., p. 286.]

She, like her husband, has her own sexual
rights; as it is through her that man is united to
the Schekhina, it is man's duty to give his wife
pleasure.

When man comes to his dwelling he must ask his wife
to grant him the favour, seeing that it is she who has
obtained for him union with the Spouse above. When
man comes back to his wife, he must ask her to grant him
her favour for two reasons: first of all, because the pleasure
of conjugal relations on returning from a journey is a
good deed, and all pleasure resulting from a good deed is
shared by the Schekhina. *We say that this pleasure constitutes a good deed* because this pleasure contributes to
the peace of the house, for thus it is written: "Thou shalt
see peace reign in thy house; thou shalt watch over it and
thou shalt not sin." What! Does man therefore sin if he
abstains from conjugal relations? Yes, truly, he commits
a sin because he undervalues the worth of the Spouse on
high, who abides with him only by reason of his union
with his wife.                      [Vol. I., p. 290.]

*Now a tradition teaches us that at the time when Rebecca was brought to the tent* of Sara, a candle was *miraculously* lighted there. *Why did this candle light itself?* Because the Schekhina came to the house at the same time as Rebecca. The mystery of this thing is as follows: The Mother on high only abides with the male when the latter has established a house by uniting with a female; it is then only that the Mother on high pours her blessing on this couple. In the same way, the Mother below abides with the male only when he has established a house by uniting with a female; then it is that the Mother below pours her blessings on this couple. Thus the male here below is encompassed by two females, as is the one above.

[Vol. I., p. 291.]

However, the *Zohar* emphasises the necessary submission of the woman. Through her, passion may invade man and deprive him of his reason. Here is the allegory, and the idea of the division of man, on a parallel with platonic and neo-platonic conceptions of the same subject.

Rabbi Yehouda says: "Man is led by three guides: by reason, the wisdom inspired by the holy soul, by passion inspired by evil inclinations, and finally by the instinct of self-preservation common to all men and called physical nature." Rab Dimé designates this last conductor of man by the name of "basis of existence." Rabbi Yehouda adds: "Note that the tempter has a hold only over the two last conductors. The guide called 'passion' does not wait for the tempter to come and seduce it; on the contrary, it runs to meet him; and this second guide bears along with him the third, which is by nature inoffensive. Such is the meaning of the words: 'And the elder said to the younger, our father is old, etc. Let us give him wine and make him drunk, and let us sleep with him.' The two daughters of Lot denote the two lower conductors of man: passion and instinct; the first guide perverts the second; passion distorts instinct. Passion is powerless to act; to accomplish evil it must have recourse to the co-operation of the body. Now the latter knows only instinct. Therefore, to attain its ends, passion begins by debasing instinct. It is then only that evil is accomplished. This is what the Scriptures mean by the words: 'And the two daughters of Lot conceived of their father.' "

[Vol. II., p. 691.]

If woman dominates, passion reigns in opposition to reason, the world is corrupted and delivered up to Justice.

The Scriptures say: "And he shall rule over thee." From henceforth, every time men yield to sin, the women on the side of Wrath (the devils) rule over them. These are the women called "turning swords," because they appear sometimes in the form of males and sómetimes in the form of females. Woe unto the world when these women rule over it! When the prophets saw the evil ways of Israel and their guilt towards the Master, they said to them: "Women loaded with riches, how can you dwell in peace when Wrath is in the world?" The Scriptures say concerning Deborah: "And she judged Israel at that time." A tradition says: Woe unto the ignorant man who is forced to have recourse to his wife to ask the blessing on the bread! What a generation was that in which Deborah lived! There was no man to judge Israel! It must needs be a woman! [Vol. V., p. 53.]

A cry that Milton was to repeat about the Britons who were led by Boadicea.

## [C] THE LEFT SIDE

*1. The Evil in God. 2. The lower world. 3. The destroyed worlds and the first races. The Rebels. 4. The necessity for prudence.*

### 1. *The Evil in God*

Just as there is in God a female element, so is there in God an evil element. Hence the origin of evil in creatures, the origin of the world of evil spirits, which are the Evil which God cast out of himself.

Therefore evil itself is inseparably bound up with good, and has the right to a certain measure of consideration and even of respect.

And in evil, as in good, there is a male element and a female element.

The spirit of evil is still a part of God, and is employed by God in special tasks. The purpose of the creation of evil spirits and beings like Cain is to mitigate evil by casting it off in the form of doomed wrong-doers, so that, without them, the creation of an endurable universe is possible.

God, foreseeing evil, at first hesitated to create; the Matrona finally persuaded him to do it, but even then he did not collaborate in all the creation.

According to another explanation put forward by the scholars, this verse of Genesis applies to herald angels. These, knowing the past and the future, and, therefore, foreseeing that man would end by sinning, opposed the creation of the man. But more than this; when the Schekhina said to the Holy One, blessed be his name, "Let us make man," the demons Aza and Azaël set themselves against the creation of man, saying "Why create man, since thou knowest that he will end by sinning against thee with his wife, who emanates from the side of *passive* light called 'darkness'? For the male emanates from the side of *active* light, while the woman emanates from the left side, where in 'the world of creation' darkness reigns." Then the Schekhina replied to them: "You set yourselves up against man, reproaching him with the woman, a woman shall be the cause of your fall, for thus it is written: 'The sons of God saw the daughters of men that they were fair; and they took them wives of all that they chose.' When these angels felt desire for women and allowed themselves to be seduced, the Schekhina cast them out and deprived them of their holiness." The learned men replied to Rabbi Simeon: "Master, the demons Aza and Azaël did not lie, however, when they said that man would end by sinning with a woman?" Rabbi Simeon replied to them: "It is for that very reason that the Schekhina said to those demons: Inasmuch as you set yourselves up against men, it behoves you to be more chaste than they. Now man will end by sinning with one woman, while you will end by sinning with several women, for thus it is written: 'The sons of God saw the daughters of men that they were fair'; the Scriptures do not speak of one daughter but of several. Moreover, said the Schekhina, man will do penance after his sin, *while you will not do so*."

The learned men said to Rabbi Simeon: "Since sexual desires are the cause of all evil, why do they exist?" Rabbi Simeon replied to his colleagues: "If the Holy One, blessed be his name, had not created the Spirit of good and the Spirit of evil, of which the one emanates from the side of light and the other from the side of darkness, man could never have deserved praise or blame; that is why God created him a composite of two spirits. Now, sexual desires are good or bad according to the spirit which inspires them; that is why the Scriptures say: 'See, I have set before you Life and Good on the one hand, and, on the other, Death and Evil.'" The colleagues replied: Why had man to merit praise or blame? Had it not been better that the spirit of good only should have been given to man and that he should merit nothing? Thus created, he would never have caused such havoc in the heavenly regions! Rabbi Simeon replied to them: It was right that man should be composed of the two afore-mentioned spirits, seeing that the law was created on his behalf; the law wills that the evil doers shall be chastised and that the righteous shall be rewarded. So that the righteous may be rewarded, the evil-doers must be punished; *now* God willed that good should be spread abroad throughout the world, for thus it is written: "God did not create the earth in vain, but fashioned it that men might dwell therein." The learned men replied to Rabbi Simeon: "We have just heard a thing that we have never before heard; for it is evident that the Holy One, blessed be his name, created nothing that was useless. But more than this. The created law constitutes the garment of the Schekhina. If man had not been created with the faculty of sinning, the Schekhina would have remained without garments like a beggar. That is why he who commits sins is as a man who strips the Schekhina of her garments, and this is what deserves punishment; and he who keeps the commandments of the Scriptures, is as worthy of praise as if he clothed the Schekhina in her garments."

[Vol. I., p. 141.]

After all these doubts and discussions, it is the Schekhina alone who created the body of man. Her rôle of mother, intermediary power and mediator is thus conceived very clearly. She has pity on her children, defends them against their enemies, intercedes for them with the Father.

... all the colleagues of Rabbi Simeon rose up and cried: "Rabbi, is there then a division between the Father and the Mother, so that man by emanation belongs to the Father and by creation to the Mother?" Rabbi Simeon replied to them: Friends, friends, such is not my meaning, since the man "of emanation" is composed of a male and a female, which emanate from the Father and from the Mother, for thus it is written: "And Elohim said: 'Let there be light, and there was light.'" *By the words* "let there be light" the Scriptures denote the part of man which emanates from the Father, *that is to say the male*, and *by the words* "and there was light" the Scriptures denote the part of man which emanates from the Mother, *that is to say the female*. That is why man was created with two faces. But the man "of emanation" is devoid of image and of likeness; and it is the heavenly Mother who wished to give the man of the "world of creation" an image and a likeness. *Now*, the two *heavenly* lights emanating from the Father and the Mother being called *in the Scriptures* "light" and "darkness," the image, *that is to say the body of man* must be equally composed of the active light, *emanating from the Father*, and of the passive light, called "darkness," *emanating from the Mother*. But as the Father had said to the Mother that man would end by sinning in the "world of creation," he refused to be associated with the Mother in the creation of the garment, *that is to say the body* of man. That is why the light created on the first day of the Creation was concealed by the Holy One, blessed be his name, for the righteous, and the darkness created on the first day of the Creation was concealed for the impious, for thus it is written: "And the impious shall be reduced to silence in their darkness." And as it is because of the darkness that man must end by sinning against the "light," the Father did not wish to be associated in the creation of the man below. That is why the Mother says to the Father: "Let us make man in our image," *that is to say* of "light" and "in our likeness," *that is to say* of passive light, so that the body serves as a garment for the soul, as it is written: "Thou hast clothed me with flesh and skin." [Vol. I., p. 137.]

There remains therefore, both in God and in the world, an unclean, evil side. God is obliged to show his anger against this category of being. Here again we find ourselves face to face with very primitive conceptions. The Schekhina proceeds from the female deities. The side of Evil, by the same effort of thought towards divine unity which had united the female to the male in a divine hermaphrodite, proceeds from the primitive idea of another god, hostile to God, the world and man. To bring about divine unity, it was necessary to make the Enemy a part of God. His expulsion gives another purpose to creation.

The stranger said to them: When the moon approaches the sun, the Holy One, blessed be his name, awakens the North and draws it unto him in love, while the South awakens of itself. Now as the sun rises in the East, it follows that he derives his strength from the two sides, both from the North and from the South, and that he silently attracts the blessings which emanate from the

two sides and transmits them to the moon which becomes
filled with them. The union of the sun and the moon
resembles that of the male and female, for the same principles which govern the elements here below are also
found in the things above. Just as the arm of the *sephirothic
tree* draws unto itself the immensity of space in love, as
the arm of the male draws the female, so does the left
arm draw the immensity of space in wrath. Now the
serpent constitutes the left arm from which emanates the
unclean spirit. It draws unto it all those who approach
it. So when God does not awaken the North, the left arm
draws the moon unto itself and clasps her so firmly that,
in order to free her, Israel is obliged to offer it a he-goat.
The serpent, rushing on the goat, just offered to it, relin-
quishes for an instant its hold on the moon, which begins
from that time to shine and wax bigger each day, because
she is then receiving the blessings from on high, which
light up her face, that has been obscured a while here
below. So during the day of pardon, as the serpent is
busy with the goat offered to it, the moon, set free, occupies herself with the defence and protection of Israel,
as a mother protects her children, after which the Holy
One, blessed be his name, blesses Israel and forgives its
sins.                                           [Vol. I, p. 374.]

According to other passages, God seems to have
been moved by a creative impulse of which he had
not complete control. One curious passage, too
long to quote, explains that God, in man's interest, left the creation of evil spirits till the last,
because he knew that the Sabbath would come and
interrupt his work. Indeed, the appointed hour
came when he had given them spirits but not yet
bodies; and the devils have no bodies. Therefore

they cannot reproduce themselves, which is a great blessing; for they would multiply and cover the earth so that man would be powerless against them.

In the following passage it is the Schekhina who puts a stop to this evil creation, by coming to tempt the Creator in a way which is quite openly sexual. A prototype of Judith, who prostituted herself to save her people, the Matrona comes and offers herself to the Lord God in order to save men imperilled by the creation of evil spirits; an extremely quaint conception, very characteristic of the primitive mentality in the *Zohar*.

We learnt, moreover, in the *Occult Book* that all wrath emanating from the male Element is harsh at first and milder towards the end, while the wrath emanating from the female Element is moderate at first and harsh towards the end. So if these two elements were to go hand in hand the world could not continue to exist. And it was with the very object of tempering the one with the other that the Ancient of Days separated them. When he separated them, the Ancient of Days caused a deep sleep to fall upon the "Little Face"; he took from him the female Element, decked her with all her ornaments and kept her for the day when he should present her to man; for thus it is written: "And the Lord God caused a deep sleep to fall upon Adam, and he slept; and he took one of his ribs and closed up the flesh instead thereof." He took the rib which is the image of wrath, and closed up the flesh, image of mercy; for thus it is written: "I will take away your heart of stone and will give you an heart of flesh." And when the Sabbath was about to begin, he (the Great Face) created the spirits of the demons and devils, but before he had finished them, the Matrona, decked with her ornaments, came and sat before him. Then he abandoned the work begun and never finished it.

When the Matrona lies with the King (143a) and is united to him, who would dare to come between them? Who would dare to draw near them? Their union appeases wrath and perfects the creatures above and below.

[Vol. V., p. 367.]

And yet it is from sexual union that evil arose. We have seen the question asked by the rabbis: *"Since sexual desires are the cause of all evil why do they exist?"* and Simeon's very unsatisfactory reply. Here are some passages which show the close though rather puzzling connection between evil and sexual life. The fact is that in everything there is a good and an evil side; a gloomy reflection never lost sight of by the cabalists.

... It is written: "I shall visit their iniquities upon them with a rod, and I shall punish their sins by divers plagues." This contains a supreme mystery. The "remembrance" and the "visit" have always a good significance when they emanate from the right side of the male or female element, but they have always a bad significance when they emanate from the left side, which constitutes the mystery expressed by the term "strange gods." This side also is composed of a male element and a female element. From the union of the two elements of the right side emanate the mystery of the Faith and the heavenly sanctities, as has been already said; while from the union of the two elements of the left side emanate all evil spirits and death, as well as all the ills which trouble the world. Thus the left side is the opposite of the right side.

[Vol. II., p. 229.]

One of the reasons for the existence of the world is the casting out of the evil beings who are part of God himself; this is why Cain was born.

We learnt, moreover, in the *Occult Book* that the Holy Ancient One, wishing to see if wrath were appeased, united the male and the female. A fierce wrath issued from the side of the woman, as it is written: "And Adam knew Eve, his wife, and she bare Cain." The world could not exist, for wrath was not appeased, and the powerful serpent had defiled it. That is why he caused Cain, that is to say fierce wrath, to come forth and thus mitigate the wrath on the woman. The Scriptures say: "When Cain and Abel were in the field"—that is to say in "the field of the apple trees," of which we have spoken, Cain (wrath) slew Abel; then the Holy One, blessed be his name, caused Cain (wrath) to disappear, and he plunged him into the abyss of the Great Ocean. [Vol. V., p. 368.]

But, in the end, mercy triumphs.

We learnt in the *Occult Book* that after the union of the sacred Man above, whose body is formed of male and female, all the worlds above and below obtained tranquillity; and after the third union, they united for all eternity and formed but one and the same body; and one only is seen, for thus it is written: "Holy, holy, holy is Jehovah Cebaoth! All the earth is full of his glory." The whole forms but one body, never a female, like a date tree growing up both male and female. The man who holds himself aloof here below from the human species will not form part, in the world to come, of the Man called the Sacred Body, but he will belong to those Spirits who are not called "man." The Scriptures say: "We will make you chains of gold inlaid with silver." These words

signify that Wrath is tempered with Mercy; there is no
wrath without mercy; that is why the Scriptures add:
"Thy cheeks are comely with rows of jewels, thy neck
with chains of gold." "Thy neck" is the Matrona who
dwells in the Sanctuary above, and in Jerusalem below,
and it is because she is united with the male that she is
confused with man. This is the quintessence of the whole
Faith; for in this mystery the whole Faith is hidden.

[Vol. V., p. 369.]

## 2. *The Lower World*

Evil and evil spirits are organised as a kingdom
in the likeness of God and his world.

Note that on the holy side there is a King and a Priest
who offers up sacrifices. There is on high a King who
constitutes the mystery of the Holy of Holies, and below
him there is a Priest called "High Priest," because he
constitutes the primitive light. But there is below yet
another King, like the King above; he rules over the
worlds below. Below him there is a priest, and this priest
is the angel Michael, the high priest of the right side.
This fact constitutes the mystery of the perfect faith. But,
like the holy side, the "other side" has also its king and
its priest. It has its king, for thus it is written: "An old
and foolish king"; and it has its priest, as it is written:
"Ephraim said: Nevertheless I have grown rich; I have
proved that the idol looked with favour on me." It was
the might of this priest that made it possible for the work
of Jereboam to endure. When the king and the priest of
the "other side" are defeated and crushed, all the forces
on that same side are defeated; and they acknowledge the
supremacy of the Holy One, blessed be his name; and

then the Holy One, blessed be his name, rules alone above and below, for thus it is written: "And the Lord God alone shall appear great on that day."

[Vol. III., p. 299.]

The King below has a Schekhina, who is known by various names, the most frequently met with being that of Lilith.

When the primitive light had been hidden, a membrane formed around the brain. This membrane, growing, produced a second one. When the latter appeared, it reached right up to the "Little Face"; it felt the desire to cleave to the Little Face, to leave its impress on it and never leave it. The Holy One, blessed be his name, separated it from the Little Face and cast it down below. When God created man, with the purpose of preparing for the advent of the Little Face in this world, the membrane, seeing Eve cleave to man, whose lovely face was the image of the one on high, recalled the perfect Face *it had formerly seen*. It flew away from the earth and tried once more to cleave to the Little Face; but the keepers of the gates above did not let it enter. The Holy One, blessed be his name, thrust it violently away and cast it into the depths of the ocean abyss. There it remained until the day Adam and his wife sinned. On that day, the Holy One, blessed be his name, made it come forth from the depths of the ocean abyss and gave it power over the children, who having little faces are liable to punishment through the sins of their forefathers. It flew throughout the world. It approached the gates of the earthly paradise, and seeing the "cherubim," who guard these gates, it sat down beside the flaming sword, for it was to a spark from this sword that it owed its birth. When it saw this sword turning, it fled and winged its way rapidly through the world; and, finding children liable to punishment, it killed them. This happened when the moon was on the wane. That is why *the word* "Meoroth" is *not written in full.* Until the birth of Cain, the membrane could not approach Adam; but afterwards it drew near him and brought forth evil spirits and winged devils. For a hundred years Adam had intercourse with the female devils until the arrival of "Naàmâ," whose beauty seduced the angels "Aza" and "Azaêl," whom the Scriptures call the "sons of God." By them she conceived and gave birth to the evil spirits and devils which swarm in the world. "Naàmâ" goes throughout the world during the night; she adorns herself and excites men to such an extent as to cause them seminal losses—wherever a man sleeps alone in a house, she cleaves to him; guilty passions are, to her, fecundating matter. She also cleaves to men when they are sick. All this takes place during the time that the moon is on the wane. [Vol. I., p. 119.]

Now the Schekhina below is mysteriously related to the Schekhina above. We come across her in our poets. Milton gave Satan a daughter-wife with whom Satan commits incest, which results in the birth of a dire spirit, Death. Hugo also makes use of Lilith; and his conception of the Angel Liberty, who is the daughter of Satan and who is to save the world, emphasises the connection between the two Schekhinas.

It was owing to the crime of incest that Israel went into captivity with the Schekhina, in whom he had uncovered that which should be hidden. . . . . . . . .
. . . . . . . . . . . . These are the devils who separate the two Hés and prevent the Vav from coming in

between; that is why the Scriptures say: "Thou shalt not uncover in the woman and her daughter that which should be hidden"; this is an allusion to the Intruders, consisting of "Nephilim, Ghiborim, Amalequim, Rephaim and Anaquim," who interposed themselves between the two Hés; and as long as they are there, the Holy One, blessed be his name, refuses to approach. This mystery is expressed in the words of the Scriptures: "The river shall be dried up and barren," *that is to say*, the Hé above, *the symbol of the Schekhina above*, shall be dried up, and the Hé below, *the symbol of the Schekhina below*, shall be barren to prevent the Intruders from feeding on the Vav which is the tree of Life. That is why the Vav does not come near the two Hés as long as the Intruders are there; and the Holy One, blessed be his name, symbolised by the Yod, forbids himself union with the final Hé of Jehovah.                              [Vol. I., p. 173.]

Man, of course, plays his part in the struggle between good and evil; and it is through his sin that evil becomes so widespread in the world. The *Zohar* points out, in reference to this (all things are in all things), the kinship of men and animals.

The beauty of the face is but rarely revealed. Certain letters composing the face are visible but others remain hidden from the beings above and below. "And God said: 'Let the earth bring forth the living creature after his kind, cattle and creeping thing,'" etc. Elsewhere the Scriptures say: "Thou succourest both man and beast, O Lord God." Man and beast have much in common; man is contained in the beast, and the beast is contained in man. When "Adam" came here below (178*b*), the heavenly

Face had two spirits, the one on the right side intended
for man, and the other on the left side intended for animals.
But after the sin of Adam, the left side stretched out so far
that it even entered man. The result of this was a surplus
of the spirit of the right side, which was no longer able
to find any part of man's body to enter, the other spirit
having taken its place. Hence the mingling of the two
spirits, of which monsters are begotten. Although the
twenty-two letters are hidden above, they are visible here
below. There is also a hidden Yod as well as a visible
Yod. The Vav, which resembles the index of a pair of
scales, holds them in equilibrium. The Yod alone denotes
the male Element. The Hé denotes the female Element.
From the union of Yod and Hé issued the Vav. That is
why the Scriptures say: "The sons of God saw the daughters of men that they were fair," etc. *The term* "Daughters of men . . ." denotes the devil, for thus it is written:
(*b*) "Two harlots presented themselves before the King."
The angels, of whom the Scriptures speak, having seen
on high the supreme union of the male and female, wished
to imitate it, and they lay with the devil's harlot. Therefore they were deposed, losing the rank they had held
before.                                   [Vol. IV., p. 142.]

So the spirits of Evil imitate the powers of Good.
There is, mingled with all the good and divine
relationship between the various worlds of the
Cabala, an evil relationship. But this is inevitable.

And even among the Sephiroth, each desires to increase by drawing unto her the supreme wisdom. And
in spite of his perfection, Jacob could not wholly escape
from the envy between the two worlds. But when other
men imitate the action of Jacob, they provoke hatred,

causing separation, and lay bare, above as well as below, what shame requires should be concealed. It is in this theory that the mystery concerning incest is hidden. Men who act thus lay bare that which should remain hidden in mother and daughter. [Vol. IV., p. 4.]

Here, finally, is another attempt to justify the existence of evil: *the spirit of evil does the will of his master*. Note that this inclines towards the idea that it is necessary to a certain extent to pander to evil. This is an idea that we shall find again

But, it may be urged, how can man love God when the spirit of evil is seeking all the time to estrange man from the service of God? The love of God actually consists in subduing the spirit of evil, in breaking its might and in winning it over to the service of the Holy One, blessed be his name. This mystery is known to the initiated. All that the Holy One, blessed be his name, made, above and below, had but one purpose, that of proclaiming his glory; all things were made but to do his will. Now can we imagine a slave rebelling against his master and thwarting his will? The will of God is that men should devote themselves constantly to his service, and walk in the way of truth, so that they may be deemed worthy of manifold rewards. As such is the will of God, how can a bad slave come to thwart his master's will, lead men into the wrong path, turn men aside from the right path, and finally persuade them not to do the will of their master? But the truth is that the spirit of evil does do the will of his master.

The thing may be compared to a king who had an only son whom he loved greatly. He exhorted his son not to consort with any wicked woman, for whoever consorts with such a one is not worthy to enter the king's palace. The son promised to obey his father's wishes. Outside the palace was a courtesan of great physical beauty and charm. One day the king said to himself: "I desire to see if my son is obeying my will." He summoned the courtesan and said to her: "Strive to seduce my son; for I desire to see how far he obeys my will." The courtesan set about following the king's son, embracing and kissing him, and putting forth all her arts of seduction. As the son is upright and attentive to his father's exhortation, he does not hearken unto the courtesan but casts her off. The king then rejoices with his son, makes him enter his palace, showers presents on him and covers him with glory. Now who is the cause of all this glory of the son? Is it not the courtesan who deserves twofold praise: first, because she did but obey the king's commands, and secondly, because she is the cause of all the glory with which the king covered his son? That is why the destroying angel, *who is none other than the spirit of evil*, is called "very good," because he is the occasion of much good to him who listens to the voice of his master. Note that were it not for this spirit, the righteous would not inherit the heavenly treasures in store for them in the world to come. Happy are those who withstand this spirit. It is well that many withstand him and that others obey him. For those who withstand him shall be rewarded and those who obey him shall be cast into hell and effaced from the world of the living. But of what use is it that many should obey him (163*b*)? It is because in this way he is strengthened. Just as a murderous evil doer finds no rest until he has killed a man, so the spirit of evil, who is one with the destroying angel, only renews his strength when he has led astray or killed a man. [Vol. IV., p. 105.]

## 3. *The Destroyed Worlds and the First Races*

The evil side of God is, to a certain extent, bound up with the history of the times before creation. God had first of all created worlds which did not satisfy him. He destroyed them; their ruins form chaos. But some evil spirits, however, survive.

These primitive beings did not reproduce themselves by the same process as the beings of this world, and had no knowledge of our sexual life. Therefore they were not made in the image of God and had to disappear.

These were the mysterious kings, the unknown races of Gog and Magog.

All these kings are on the side of Wrath, save Saul who is of Rehoboth-Lanahar, symbol of "Bina"; whence open the fifty "doors of Intelligence" in the four directions of the world.

These kings, who were on the side of Wrath, were only appeased by the coming of "Hadar." Who is "Hadar"? He is heavenly grace, as the Scriptures add: "His town was called Phaii," which means that it is through God that man receives the Holy Spirit. The Scriptures further add: "And his wife was called Mehetabel, daughter of Matred, who was the daughter of Mezaab. He is the first king who is said to have had a wife. "Matred" signifies that wrath was tempered with mercy.    [Vol. V., p. 366.]

Sometimes these kingdoms are of the pre-Adam era; sometimes these beings belong to an early Adam period, or spring from his guilty union with the Schekhina below, the mate of the devil.

Adam was composed of male and female, and the female joined to his side was also composed of male and female, so that they might be complete. Adam looked with wisdom on the world above and on that below. After his sin, the faces withered away, and wisdom was taken from him, so that he had no intelligence left save for material and bodily things. He afterwards had children modelled on the world above and on the one below. But they were not the founders of the future generations. It was only Seth who was the founder of the future generations.

[Vol. V., p. 301.]

At times whole worlds were created and then destroyed; the remains of such worlds form that chaos which existed before our earth was made.

"And the earth was without form and void." The Scriptures mean that the children of the heavens and the earth were *the devils called* "without form." This explains the following tradition: "The Holy One, blessed be his name, created worlds and destroyed them." That is why the Scriptures say: "And the earth was without form and void"; *now the state of being without form and void existed before the creation of the earth; but that may be explained in this way: that by the word "earth" the Scriptures denote the previously existing earth, which God destroyed.* How can we believe that the Holy One, blessed be his name, created worlds to destroy them? It would have been better not to have created them! Truly, *this tradition* contains a mystery; for how otherwise can we explain the words: "and destroyed them." [Vol. I., p. 152.]

Here is one of the passages most characteristic of the style of the *Zohar* when it means to be mysterious. In it we shall find the reason for the first failures: these early beings were ignorant of the proper mode of sexual union.

We learned in the *Occult Book that, in creating the world, God weighed* in the balance *that which had not till then been weighed.* Before this time, men did not look at each other face to face, *that is to say, the union of man and wife did not take place as in these days.* So the primitive kings perished because they did not find the nourishment they required; and the earth itself was destroyed. Then the most desirable "Head" took pity on the world he was about to create. The balance was hung in a place where it had never been before. The balance weighed bodies as well as souls, and even beings which did not yet exist. As there were no beings prior to this, it was existing beings and those destined to exist later who were placed upon the balance. In this way the present world was formed; this is the Mystery of mysteries. A dew, crystal clear, fills the cavity of the "Head." The membrane which covers it is equally clear, like the air, and is mysterious. Very fine hairs hang from this balance.     [Vol. IV., p. 137.]

It is of interest here to add a few of Pauly's comments which incorporate cabalistic traditions evolved from the *Zohar*.

" . . . In the Balance."
By this expression is understood the juxtaposition of male and female in the whole work of creation. The pre-existent worlds were created only by the Yod, the male Element. Thus the union of husband and wife did not take place as in our world. Only the male acted, while the female, amounting solely to an extra face, figured merely as an adjunct to make the human body resemble the image

of God, who is equally composed of male Element (Jehovah, first hypostasis) and of female Element (Elohim,
second hypostasis); but she did not contribute in any
way to generation (*v.* Idra Rabba, Z., iii., 142*a*, id est:
coitus quo anteriorum terrarum homines non usi sunt.—
*v.* also Idra Zouta, Z., iii., 289*b*). Men born thus could not
continue to exist, because they lacked "Heavenly Grace,"
which alone watches over man and gives him the strength
needful to withstand the temptations of the "other side."
As the previous worlds were created only by the Yod,
"Heavenly Grace," which is poured out only by the Hé
(the female Element), was entirely absent. But why did
God not create previous worlds by the Hé, so that
"Heavenly Grace" might be poured forth, thus prevent-
ing their ruin? It was because the men of the previous
worlds had as souls spirits in revolt against God; they did
not therefore deserve that heaven should give them
"grace" to help them. So God put them to the test; had
they been able to withstand the temptations of the "other
side" unaided by "grace," they would have been saved.
But all succumbed and the worlds were one after the
other destroyed. Only the present world was created by
the male Element in conjunction with the female Element,
and man also is formed by the co-operation of the two.
Formerly man was made only in the image of God (two
faces); in the present world he is made in the image and
likeness of God, since man and woman co-operate in
generation (*Tiqouné Zohar*, xix.)

[Vol. VI., p. 389, n. 1442.]

There seem, however, to have been possibilities of continuance in these pre-human beings:

We learned in the *Occult Book* that the Ancient of
ancients, before preparing his ornaments, set up and
established kings; but these could not continue, and it was

141

necessary to hide them and keep their existence for a future time, as it is written: "Such were the kings who ruled over the land of Edom before the children of Israel had a king." The land of Edom denotes the place of wrath.

. . . . . . . . .

The worlds pre-existent in the supreme Thought could not last because man was not yet corporate, man whose image is the synthesis of all (355b). And when the face of man was formed, existence was assured to all creatures. If the Scriptures say, "And such a king is dead and such another king is dead," they mean that his existence was postponed to a later time, for every descent to a lower degree is called "death." He had fallen to a lower degree. When man was created, then came to an end the existence of those they bore before, save the being of whom the Scriptures say: "And his wife was called Mehetabel, daughter of Matred, who was the daughter of Mezaab." He was the only primitive being who could continue to exist, because he was composed of male and female, like a date palm, which flourishes only when the female is planted beside the male. Although this being could continue to exist in the primitive worlds, because he was formed of both male and female, he could not attain perfection until after the formation of man. [Vol. V., p. 355.]

In one special case the posterity of the pre-Adamites survived and was cast by God into hell.

(144b), p. 58, l. 18.—"Of whom Adam was the image." Taking this passage as a basis, the modern cabalists, among others the "Etz-ha-Hayim," xvi., and the Minhath Yehouda, fol. 113b, affirm that, before the creation of Adam, God had created another man, male only without female, but this did not prevent him from begetting children. As these children attached themselves of their own accord to the serpent, without even having been tempted by it, God drove them from this world and made them the guardians of hell, where they are burned up each day by the fire and reborn the next day. The cabalists designate these beings by the name of "dead kings" because of the sin against the "Holy Spirit"; for they call "sin against the Holy Spirit" any sin committed of the sinner's own accord, and not as the result of overwhelming temptation. [Vol. VI., p. 383, n. 1414.]

Here I add a passage which proves that the Christian idea that the heathen gods were devils, rebellious angels, is also to be found in the Cabala.

. . . by the expression "the gods who did not make the heavens and the earth," the Scriptures denote certain angels who, *in revolt against heaven*, pass themselves off as gods. [Vol. I., p. 52.]

## 4. *Prudence*

Evil being thus mingled with good, it behoves man to be prudent. Evil spirits have a right to his consideration; and this is an excuse for a sort of cowardice which is very human.

Just as the clean comes sometimes out of the unclean, so does the unclean at times come out of the clean. Thus although the "red cow" may have served for a sacred rite, those who had to do with it are declared unclean and have need of purification. Rabbi Simeon then said to him: The unclean spirit must be subdued wherever it is possible to do so. I wish to reveal to you a mystery

143

which must be revealed only to very saintly men. The
Holy One, blessed be his name, gave to the unclean spirit
power to extend his dominion in the world and to lay
waste wherever he could do so. But we are not authorised
to treat him with scorn; we must be on our guard that
he does not attack us when we are engaged in holy things.
Therefore, in all our good works we should leave a small
place for the devil, so that he may not defile our whole
work. Does not his power come from the holy side? Why
then should we not accord him his part in the holy works
that we perform? That is why the edges of our phy-
lacteries are provided with a hair, so that the devil may
cling to it; it is his share in this holy work. The purpose
of the scape-goat was the same. Happy is the man whose
works are undefiled save in the part he has himself left
for the devil; so that the latter shall not accuse him above
and bring down evil upon him.          [Vol. IV., p. 265.]

According to the same principle, error and
foolishness have their place by the side of wisdom;
and here is one of the choicest passages in the
*Zohar*. The rabbis who collaborated in the evolution of cabalistic ideas were certainly the first to
apply these principles, and that right zealously.

As to the words, "And I saw that wisdom prevails
over foolishness," they mean that wisdom derives an
advantage from foolishness. A tradition teaches us that it
is part of the duty of a man who teaches wisdom to make
his listeners acquainted, at the same time, with a little
foolishness, because wisdom profits from foolishness just
as light profits from darkness, since, were it not for darkness, we should not know light or understand its usefulness. Rabbi Simeon said to Rabbi Abba: "Light from

above is shed only while foolishness, emanating from another region, is being diffused here below in the same measure." It is therefore due to foolishness that we receive the light of wisdom. The venerable Rabbi Hammenouna was wont to let his listeners hear something of foolishness while he was teaching them the mysteries of wisdom, so that the students should thus acquire a better appreciation of wisdom. Black teaches us to value white, bitter to value sweet. That is why the Scriptures say: "The Lord God set up one side on the model of the other." And elsewhere (48a): "It is right that thou shouldst grasp one side without at the same time losing hold of the other."

[Vol. V., p. 132.]

## [D] REINCARNATION: THE QUEST OF THE TWIN-SOUL

The destinies of man cannot be fulfilled in one existence only on this earth. Difficulties arise in the search for the twin soul, in the reconstitution of the primitive unity of man, which recreates the primitive unity of God.

Hence reincarnation and its endless complications, which occupy a considerable place in the Cabala. Only a few examples of the speculations of the *Zohar* on this subject can be given here.

Souls which, here below, pass into the bodies of animals take on the shape of the garment covering them, the shape of the clean animals *enumerated in the Scriptures*: the ox, ewe, kid, stag, wild goat, buffalo, antelope, roebuck, oryx, or giraffe. Thus, as soon as spirits, *created* to be covered with a human body, are clad in the body of an animal, they take on its name. Therefore we speak of the flesh of the ox, *because the spirit residing within the ox has the shape and name of the ox*. The ox is the spirit residing within this body, while the flesh is only the garment of this spirit; and so it is with *all other animals*. That is why the spirits of the other (heathen) peoples, emanating from the side which is not holy, have not the name of man. That is also why these unclean spirits have nothing in common with the one in the midst who bears the name of man. The bodies of the heathen, which form the garments of their spirits, are called unclean flesh, seeing that the unclean spirit residing within defiles the body surrounding it. That is why the bodies of the heathen are unclean only as long as the spirits still reside within them, but as soon as the spirits have left them they are no longer unclean, and being but garments, they no longer bear the name of the spirits they clothed. The spirits of the heathen which migrate here below take on the shapes of the unclean animals enumerated in the Scriptures, in the chapter on unclean animals, such as the hog.     [Vol. I., p. 125.]

Every soul which has sinned during its passage through this world is, as a punishment, obliged to migrate as many times as is necessary to attain, when perfect, the sixth degree of the region from which it emanates. But what has just been said applies only to the souls emanating from the side of Metraton who is the "Servitor" and who encompasses the six directions. As for the souls emanating from the side of the Schekhina, who constitutes the seventh heavenly degree, they are never subject to transmigration.
[Vol. III., p. 377.]

The souls of wives at times become husbands, and those of husbands at times become wives. The twin soul destined to become the spouse of another becomes at times its mother. The soul destined to animate the brother of a certain individual at times animates his father. This is what constitutes the greatest of all miracles. That the father's soul should come down at times from heaven to effect the redemption of that of his son is comprehensible, but that the brother's soul should be transformed into the father's soul is truly marvellous. The world here below is upside down. He whom we believe to be the ancestor is in reality the descendant, and he whom we believe to be the descendant is in reality the ancestor. [Vol. III., p. 406.]

Now souls animating males emanate from the "Tree of Knowledge" which is the male Element, while souls animating females emanate from the "lower Tree" which is the female Element. A man who dies childless injures his soul; for it cannot now rise to the higher world, the degree of Joseph, where stands the "Tree of Knowledge." To save this soul, the mother, sacrificing herself, makes a fresh descent to earth, but in the form of a son, while the son's soul comes down again in the form of a mother. It goes, as a supplementary soul, to animate the body of a girl and gives birth to a son who is animated as a supplementary soul, by the soul of the mother. *The descent of the mother and the transformation of the male soul into the female and vice-versa* is absolutely indispensable in such a case, seeing that the soul of a childless man can never again come down into the body of a man, since it has no twin soul to serve as its spouse here below. For every man who dies childless is separated for ever from his spouse; his soul will never more unite with hers. This transformation of male soul into female is so painful that, if men could realise it, they would understand that no physical pain can equal it.          [Vol. III., p. 408.]

If a man takes a wife but has no children, his existence here below is considered as null and void. His soul returns to the world of the male Element and his wife's to that of the female Element. But this happens only in the case of a man who had no children because he did not wish for them, or because the woman did not wish for them. But where sterility is not due to the unwillingness of the couple, the souls of such couples come back on earth a second time. It also happens sometimes that after his return here below a man, as a result of prayers to Heaven, weds a woman whose soul is not his twin soul. In this case the man derives no merit from his marriage or paternity, since the woman he married is not his twin soul. The children he has by this woman are credited rather to the man who was the woman's twin soul, whom the children's apparent father had ousted by his prayers. This man is like one who cultivates the garden of another; the owner of the garden alone enjoys its fruits, he who cultivated them does not do so. Such is the meaning of the words: "And if his master causes him to wed a woman by whom he has sons and daughters, the woman and her children shall belong to the woman's master; while he himself shall go forth alone." But if this be so, where then is heavenly justice? Was it not the Holy One, blessed be his name, who gave this garden to the man that he might cultivate it? Why then should he be deprived of its fruits, and why should these be assigned to another?

[Vol. III., p. 429.]

It is certain that a man who comes down a second time here below is not perfect; for, if he were, his soul would not have been subjected to the penalty of transmigration. Then, if an imperfect man, such as this one, is predestined to have no children by the woman whose soul is the twin of his, he will be inevitably obliged, if he marries this woman, to return to earth a third time. But the Holy One, blessed be his name, has pity upon certain souls, and spares them the penalty of a third descent upon the earth, and this is what happens to them: instead of desiring the woman animated by a twin soul to his own, the man lets his choice fall on a woman, who is a stranger to his soul, and, as a result of prayers to Heaven, he obtains her in marriage. He then cultivates the garden of another, and the children he has are credited to the true, predestined husband of the woman, to him whose soul is the twin of the woman's. When he reaches heaven, the man hears himself condemned to descend once more upon the earth, for not having left children during his previous life, *those he had not belonging to him but to the ousted husband*. The man then protests and says: "I love my master and I desire to remain near him for evermore; I love also my wife and children and do not wish them to belong to another man." And he ends his protest with the words: "I do not wish to go forth." The Holy One, blessed be his name, then remits this soul's penalty of a new descent to earth. He summons it before a heavenly tribunal which inflicts punishment on it for the expiation of its sins. It remains without until the jubilee year and then it is allowed to enter the heavenly school. [Vol. III., p. 431.]

## III. FOLKLORE, INDIA,
## THE HERMES TRISMEGISTUS

The Cabala has brought us very near to folk-lore. No doubt, a considerable part of this hotch-potch was made up of popular beliefs more or less officially rejected by orthodoxy, but preserved and elaborated by minds of the "occultist" type.

It is of interest now to go straight to folklore and to give primitive examples of the conceptions with which we are dealing here. We shall thus see better the fundamental kinship of all these minds: primitives, occultists, poets, and the comparison of them will help us to the better understanding of all.

The kernel of all these notions, the most fundamental idea, the one most in harmony with the soul of the poet as well as with the mind of the savage, is the conception of sexual life animating the world. If there is anywhere a knot which keeps together in some sort of unity the heteroclite assortment of ideas with which we are concerned, we find it here. The world was created by a sexual act. Hence a male element, the superior one, and a female element, the inferior one. The fruit of creation issues from the female. It is therefore not the superior God who creates, he is the one that begets; the demiurge, the creator of the substance of which the world is made, is therefore the secondary God. Thus the other main ideas of the primitive conception of the world can be grouped naturally round this central one.

In one of the crudest passages of the *Zohar*, which, if judged by the very elementary style, is doubtless one of the most ancient, we saw the clear expression of this idea. *And he who is on high is the father of all; he it is who created all things. It is he who fertilised the earth which grew big and brought forth "fruits"* (tholdoth) (*Zohar*, vol. i., p. 268).

Without going over the ideas examined by all the ethnographers on reincarnation or kinship with animals, I will content myself with giving Frazer's evidence on the chief point. We saw that the Cabala declared that the union of the sexes in mankind brought about the union of the sexes in the Deity and in the world. Here is the corresponding idea, first of all in Europe:

"Our rude forefathers personified the powers of vegetation as male and female, and attempted, on the principle of homeopathic or imitative magic, to quicken the growth of trees and plants . . . the marriage of trees and plants could not be fertile without the real union of the human sexes."

". . . In the Leti, Sarmata, and some other groups of islands which lie between the western end of New Guinea and the northern part of Australia the heathen population regard the sun as the male principle by whom the earth or female principle is fertilised."

"In some parts of Java, at the season when the bloom will soon be on the rice, the husbandman and his wife visit the fields by night and engage in sexual intercourse, for the purpose of promoting the growth of the crop."*

And Frazer describes festivals whose purpose is to extort from grandfather Sun rain, food, and drink in abundance, as well as cattle, children and riches.† We have seen rain considered as the seed of the divine male. We see, in our poets, the Sun identified with God. The ideas developed by Fludd and adopted by Milton are closely related to these primitive conceptions. In the primitives and in our ultra-civilised poets, the way of "feeling" the world is the same.

One form of these same doctrines, in a somewhat further stage of evolution than among the savages, is to be found in the *Brahmanas* of India, and it is interesting to come upon them there, because in India as in the Cabala these beliefs have become the basis of very lofty metaphysical speculations. One finds in the *Brahmanas* (Satapatha and Aitareya) the story of Prajapati, the creator of the world, and his daughter Ushas.

"Prajapati conceived a passion for his own daughter. . . . May I pair with her! Thus thinking he united with her."‡
"The lord of beings was the Master of the house, and

* Frazer, *The Golden Bough* (one volume edition), ch. xi., pp. 135 136.
† Frazer, *The Golden Bough*, ch. xi., pp. 135, 136.
‡ *Sacred Books of the East*, vol. xii., pp. 208-209.

Ushas was the mistress . . . the lord of beings . . . laid seed into Ushas. There a boy was born in a year."*

This son is Agni, who may be identified with the world:

"That boy entered into the forms one after another; for one never sees him as a mere boy, but one sees those forms of his, for he assumed those forms one after another."†

As is explained elsewhere, this refers to the creation of the different kinds of animals by the union of Prajapati and Ushas. Ushas takes the female forms and Prajapati the male forms.‡

Now Ushas is the issue of Prajapati, is part of him, and an invocation to him runs thus:

"May these two, Heaven and Earth, the all-shaped, come to me! for Prajapati is Heaven and Earth. May Father and Mother come to me! for Prajapati is both father and mother!"§

We are now, therefore, dealing with the divine Hermaphrodite, who divides himself into male and female, then fecundates himself and thus produces the world, as in the Cabala. And the natural consequence of these conceptions is, as in neo-

* *Sacred Books of the East*, vol. xli., p. 158.
† *Sacred Books of the East*, vol. xli., p. 161.
‡ *Aitareya Brahmana*, iii., 33, quoted in *S.B.E.*, vol. xii., p. 284 *n.*
§ Vol. xli., p. 28.

platonism and the Cabala, the theory of the re-constitution of the Total God, who divided himself up into creatures, by the reassembling of the separated fragments.

"By offering up his own self in sacrifice, Prajapati becomes dismembered, and all those separated limbs and faculties of his come to form the universe, all that exists, from the gods . . . down to the worm, the blade of grass and the smallest particle of inert matter. It requires a new, and ever new sacrifice to build the dismembered lord of creatures up again."*

This reconstitution is carried out by Agni, and the ceremonies of the sacrifice are the reconstitution of Prajapati.

"The real purport of all sacrificial performances is the restoration of the dismembered Lord of Creatures and the reconstruction of the all."†

Another stage of these same ideas is found in the *Hermes Trismegistus*. But while Hindu mythology did not influence our poets until the eighteenth century, the influence of the *Hermes* is a direct one as early as the Renaissance. Through the *Hermes*, the weight of classical antiquity and of learned and mysterious Egypt came to reinforce these conceptions, just as, through the Cabala, they were reinforced by the immense spiritual

* *S.B.E.*, vol. xliii., pp. xvii. to xxi.
† *S.B.E.*, vol. xliii., p. xix.

power of an inspired exegesis of the sacred books of Christianity.

Some quotations from the *Hermes Trismegistus.* published in 1554 and translated as early as 1471 by Ficino, suffice to show the parallelism of this influence and of that of the Cabala:

The intelligence, the male and female god who is life and light, produces by His word another intelligence, God of Fire and Fluid.*

Man is male and female, like his father.†

The cycle being over, the universal knot was untied . . . for all animals, at first double-sexed, were divided up, simultaneously with men, and then were formed on the one side the males, on the other the females.‡

Since the World is the second god, an immortal animal, no part of a living immortal animal can ever die. Everything is a part of the world, and especially Man, the reasonable animal. The First of Beings is the eternal, the increate, God the creator of all things; the Second is made in His image, it is the world, which he engendered, which he upholds, and nourishes; the world received immortality from its father; it lives for ever.§

Soul is one, matter is one, life is one.‖

That is why, O Asclepios, and that is how all beings have two sexes.—You say that of God, then, O Trismegistus?—Not only of God, but of all beings, animate and inanimate."**

In these few lines is found complete justification for all possible ideas about the supreme God,

---

* *Menard*, p. 6.    † *Menard*, p. 8.    ‡ *Menard*, p. 9.
§ *Menard*, p. 48.    ‖ *Menard*, p. 75.    ** *Menard*, p. 141

who delegates his power to a secondary God, about the sexual law, pantheism, light and fire; the *Hermes* is equally full of theories about reincarnation, and in *Il Penseroso* Milton was able to sing of his occult studies and boast:

> Let my lamp at midnight hour
> Be seen in some high lonely bower,
> Where I may oft out watch the Bear
> With thrice great Hermes—

Hermes gave him the true doctrine, whose full development was to come to him through the Cabala.

# IV

## THE FUNCTION OF PHILOSOPHICAL
## POETRY

HAVING thus more or less defined the character
and the place of philosophical poetry, there remains
one question to be considered. What is the value
of philosophical poetry? What is the use of this
form of art in the general scheme of human life?
Philosophical poetry plays a very special part
between philosophy and religion and science. It
may now be said that what was once called "philosophy" no longer exists. The name has remained
as a general label covering various kinds of researches such as sociology, psychology, logic, etc.
Nothing corresponds any longer to what, scientifically speaking, formed the connecting link—
metaphysics. Now metaphysics undeniably expressed some essential needs of the human soul;
the modern mind has reluctantly cast it off because metaphysics, of necessity, presented, with
an accuracy which rendered them unacceptable,
ideas which have only an indefinable existence,
which are only suppositions, not even hypotheses,
which often admit of contradiction without being
shaken by it. Metaphysics carried into the scientific
realm conceptions which really belong to the
domain of the will. These metaphysical ideas can-

not claim to have a place in science, but is that a reason for refusing to consider them? They belong to another order of truth: artistic truth. They are in a latent condition only, in a state of possibility. They cannot certainly be given any positive value, but these non-true ideas have played too great a part in history for us to be able to neglect them in the future. They are the results of certain forces within us which it is better to know and look in the face: in that way they are less dangerous, they are less deceptive. For they are deceptive: if they remain in a semi-conscious state they may colour and falsify even those of our works which are most scientific in method and ambition.

We should try and consider them from a point of view which was that of our old master Plato when he launched out into myths: "possibly, nay certainly, this is not true, but there is something more or less like it which is true." They are strange ambassadors coming from inaccessible realms. Let us regard them with suspicion, but with respect; with respect, but with suspicion, somewhat as the kings of the West formerly received the envoys of the Mongol emperors.

Philosophical poetry enables us toarrive at this point of view. Plato is the father both of philosophers and of poets that are interested in ideas. He made use of myth as the poets do. Why have the highest intellects as well as the lowest so often had recourse to myth—Milton and Goethe, as well as Plato? Why were they not completely satisfied with science or philosophy? Because there is something in man which goes beyond exact science. All poetry, all great art, all higher culture, all civilisation, in fact, has been based on some sort of metaphysics, because that element of aspiration towards something which is not of this world is one of the fundamental powers of the human soul. Now Renan, with his long and subtle experience of the religious mind, could say: "Never has man when in possession of a clear idea converted it into a myth." A myth expresses an aspiration, an intuition, if we may make use of this dangerous word. The danger of taking myth seriously is obvious to all; and yet the need for it is a constant historical fact. Philosophical poetry reconciles the existence and development of myth with the knowledge that it is only myth and not reality. For in the realm of art doubt need not have a sterilising or withering effect. Poetry is carried into a region which is far beyond truth and error, which is sounder and more necessary than being beyond good and evil. In order that myths may be beneficial, they must be accompanied by two contrary convictions: one must know that they are necessary and one must know that they are false. In this way can satisfaction be given, as far as possible, to the fundamental "intuitions" of the human soul. As Blake says:

"Displaying the Eternal Vision, the Divine Similitude which if man ceases to behold he ceases to exist."

Finally, philosophical poetry makes a criticism of religion from the only point of view, perhaps, which is legitimate: the artistic point of view. The poet passes judgment on religious ideas and accepts or rejects them according to the richness of their content or of their possibilities of beauty and harmony. He thus gives us a precious commentary on religions, which he alone can give. And if we extend this way of looking at things into history, the philosophical poet becomes the representative of modern humanity amid the mass of conceptions belonging to past humanity. We have spoken of the "primitives." If "intuition" really exists, it must exist especially in the "primitive" periods of humanity. But who will interpret these conceptions, where the absurd and the grotesque are mingled with what may be "intuition"? Who will tell us what is profitable there and what is the creation of rude, undeveloped intelligences? Surely the poets, who, armed with the most refined modern culture, have yet retained enough sympathy with the elementary type of human mind to extract something valuable, perhaps, from its first impressions and reactions. As our knowledge of the primitives grows, we shall better understand the ultimate thought of the philosophical poets. As our analysis of the philosophical poets grows more definite, we shall better comprehend the deep meaning of primitive beliefs, the power which made it possible for them to subsist in their rude forms in the midst of highly developed civilisations and among subtle races, in ancient Egypt and throughout the whole history of India.

But this usefulness of philosophical poetry "beyond the true and the false" is not its whole function. There is a whole range of facts which are not at present accessible to exact science: all the subtler psychological facts of refined human thought and feeling. Psychology is still only in its infancy, and as soon as one tries to understand the subtleties of complicated feelings, it is practically of no assistance whatever. These subtle and sometimes powerful variations of human feelings and desires, which have such an important place in our life, are represented by literature and, in literature, especially by poetry. Artists, writers, poets observed and experimented long before scientists; their art, when it is sincere, is based on experience just as much as the most exact sciences claim to be. But this experience is so varied, so complex and subtle that it does not allow of the dogmatic assertions of pseudo-science. It is, none the less, experience which can be observed and is for us of the first importance. The philosophical poets have then in this non-scientific observation of man a separate class of varied and fine material to use for their airy structures. And this type of observation is part of the indispensable patrimony of mankind, being none other than the application of the ancient maxim "Know Thyself." It is only the philosophical poets who can legitimately use this very special quality of materials and bring light into this type of experience, the special domain of humanity.

Moreover, right expression is the necessary basis for exact explanation. Poets are, by nature and tradition, name-givers to things subtle. Thus they bring into intellectual life an element of precision which is peculiar to them: to express is to analyse. And the philosophical poets are armed by their artistic faculties to meet the subtleties of human nature which the philosophers can hardly be expected to consider.

That is why, then, it is good to make a close study of philosophical poetry. We find in our poets the expression, become legitimate because it has abandoned its dogmatic pretensions, of the metaphysical needs of man. We find in them an adequate criticism, from the artistic and sentimental point of view, that is to say a criticism on their own special lines, of the beliefs and traditions of humanity from their origin; and, finally, we find in them criticism and organisation of the most subtle and important human experience: the cultivation of the knowledge of ourselves in the domain of the higher inclinations.

# V

# THE PHILOSOPHICAL IDEAS OF
# EDMUND SPENSER

## I. SPENSER'S IDEAS

### I

T H E innermost source of Spenser's philosophical ideas lies in his nature, in his sensibility. One finds in *The Faërie Queene* a body of conceptions about nature which are, in reality, barely intellectualised feelings. In order to express them, Spenser made use of the most prevalent philosophical commonplaces of his time: a somewhat vague distinction between substance and form; a conception of primitive chaos; an idea, only very faintly philosophical, of reincarnation (in a few stanzas) and a rather half-hearted hope of seeing the coming of the kingdom of God (in two or three more stanzas); that is practically his whole stock of ideological learning. The contents of his numerous allegories are found to be almost worthless from the philosophical point of view;* the very most one can hold on to is that conception of reason opposed to passion, found in Book Two, which greatly

---

* I am entirely of the opinion of M. Legouis, who maintains that allegorical forms were of little interest to Spenser, who introduced them to please his friends; his real subject is certainly the "Faerie" matter. Legouis, *Spenser*, p. 98.

163

impressed Milton and which was enough to make him proclaim Spenser "a better teacher than Scot or Aquinas." This very conception is, moreover, also one of the commonplaces of the day. The neo-platonism in the two first hymns, taken for the most part from Ficino's Commentary on the *Banquet*, has in reality no place in *The Faërie Queene*,* nor even in the two last hymns. It may be considered as a rhetorical exercise, in which there is no original thought, which Spenser, prompted by a fine spirit of contradiction, printed with the two last hymns, while at the same time repudiating it; doubtless with the pride of a man of letters who cannot bear to see one of his most successful literary efforts lost.

But, on the other hand, if, properly speaking, Spenser's philosophical ideas are vague and few and far between, there exists in his poems, especially in *The Faërie Queene*, a considerable amount of philosophical "feeling." Feelings, which are the starting point of metaphysical cogitation, are very strong in Spenser, and constitute poetic material of very great value. They may be presented in two groups, which, together, form the very substance of his philosophy—if we may now

* Notwithstanding the efforts of Miss Winstanley in her essay on "Spenser and Plato" (Introduction to her edition of the Hymns), the "platonism" of the virtues allegorised by Spenser appears to be very superficial; in any case it applies only to the ethics, which are themselves without interest, philosophically or otherwise.

use this convenient term since we have just made reservations about it.

Following the natural order of these feelings, the first group includes: the feeling that nature is alive; the feeling that nature is fruitful; the association of sensuality with the feeling for nature; the lively sense of the vicissitudes of nature. This latter feeling is related to the second group which may be described as a very keen sense of the vicissitudes of human destiny and of the course of the world in general.

These feelings are not indeed peculiar to Spenser; we are, in fact, specially concerned in this study with discovering in him a fairly typical instance of the formation of poetic philosophy. Perhaps, however, to him, with his acute sensibility, heightened by countless personal disappointments, the feeling of the mutability of things was more terrible than to most other poets. Milton, for instance, who feels as keenly as Spenser the painful adversities of life, is affected by them less permanently, and more easily finds refuge in hope and faith and eternal justice.

## 2. THE FEELING FOR NATURE IN SPENSER

A real feeling for nature exists in Spenser. To be sure, it is not developed to its fullest extent; it occupies little actual space in *The Faërie Queene*, and a large part of even this space is taken up with imitations of the classical writers, of Chaucer, the Italians or the French Pleiade.* But the feeling is undeniably strong, however, even in the imitations. One imitates, moreover, only what one admires, and consequently, up to a certain point, only what one is in sympathy with.

The forest, the usual background for knightly adventures, is often awesome and perilous, but it is also often gracious and smiling; and it is in this friendly and protective mood that it appears at our first introduction to it. Una and the knight seek shelter there from the storm:

A shadie grove not far away they spide
That promist ayde the tempest to withstand;
Whose loftie trees, yclad with sommers pride
Did spread so broad, that heavens light did hide
Not perceable with power of any star
And all within were paths and alleies wide . . .
And forth they passe, with pleasure forward led,
Joying to hear the birds sweet harmony. . . .

* See, on this point, Moorman, *The Interpretation of Nature in English Poetry from Beowulf to Shakespeare* (Strasbourg, 1905), and Schramm, *Spenser's Naturschilderungen* (Leipzig, 1908). I take my examples from the *Faërie Queene*, especially, because it is there that the "philosophical" feelings are chiefly to be found. I am not making here a general study of Nature in the works of Spenser, but I am only looking at things from this particular angle.

Much can they praise the trees so straight and high,
The sayling pine, the cedar proud and tall. . . .

A great part of this feeling seems artificial to us;
it consists, according to the traditional manner of
rhetoric, in attributing human feelings to natural
objects. But to Spenser, nevertheless, nature has
the same feelings as mankind and pulsates with a
life similar to human life. This is much more
strongly marked in the description of the two en-
chanted trees at the end of Canto II. (Book I.),
though the manner here is even more artificial:

Plast in open plaines
Where Boreas doth blow full bitter bleake,
And scorching sunne does dry my secret vaines;
For though a tree I seeme yet cold and heat me
    paines.*

The feeling for nature is more normal in this little
picture of a knight taking his ease:

He feedes upon the cooling shade and bayes
His sweatie forehead in the breathing Wynd
Which through the trembling leaves full gently
    playes,
Wherein the cherefull birds of sundry kynd
Doe chaunt sweet musick, to delight his mynd.†

* *F.Q.*, I. 2, 33.          † *F.Q.*, I. 7, 3.

If delights are mingled with natural charms in
the description of the garden to which Phaedria
takes Cymochles, it is the beauties of nature which
conduce to these delights:

It was a chosen plott of fertile land,
Emongst wide waves sett like a little nest,
As if it had by natures cunning hand
Bene choycely picked out from all the rest;
No daintie flowre or herbe that growes on grownd
No arborett with painted blossoms drest
And smelling sweet, but there it might be found
To bud out faire and throwe her sweet smels al
       around,
No tree, whose branches did not bravely spring,
No branch, whereon a fine bird did not sitt,
No bird, but did her shrill notes swetly sing,
No song, but did contain a lovely ditt.*

As Spenser tells us in the following stanza,
these are certainly "false delights and pleasures,"
but, firstly, the condemnation applies to the delights and not to Nature herself, and, secondly, the
fact remains that the poet is sensible of the charm
he expresses so harmoniously. And this is equally
true of the description of the sea in Canto XII. of
the same book:

* II. 6, 12 and 13.

With that the rolling sea resounding soft
In his big base them fitly answered;
And on the rocke the waves breaking aloft
A solemne meane unto them measured;
The whiles sweet zephyrus lowd whisteled
His treble, a strange kind of harmony;
Which Guyons senses softly tickeled
That he the boteman bad row easily,
And let him heare some part of their rare melody.*

These examples, of which more could be given
(though they do not very frequently occur), suffice
to show that Spenser was keenly alive to the beauties of nature, and that nature was to him essentially a living thing, stirred by winds, perfumed
by fragrant scents, filled with the song of birds
and with resounding harmonies.

This Nature of his is extraordinarily fruitful;
and when Spenser speaks of "the great earths-
wombe"† he is hardly using a metaphor. The
beings closest to her are not repugnant. Wild
creatures know how to sympathise, at times, with
man's misfortunes: Una's lion, for instance, and
the dove which, in Canto VIII. of Book IV., brings
pity and help to the "gentle squire" in love with
Belphoebe. The satyrs, too, treat Una with respect, and, apart from habits peculiar to them
(professional ones, so to speak), they are neither

* II. 12, 33.　　　† II. 1, 60.

repellent nor cruel. Sir Satyrane forms a curious link between these, the animals and mankind; son of a satyr and a mortal, he is lord of all the beasts in the forest.

> He would learne
> The Lyon stoup to him in lowly wise
> (A lesson hard) and make the libbard sterne
> Leave roaring . . .
> That his behest they feared, as a tyrans law.

He comes back from time to time, not being in any way ashamed of his origin:

> To seeke his kindred, and the lignage right
> From whence he tooke his well deserved name
> To see his syre and offspring auncient.

This is because he is "of beastly kind," which does not, however, prevent him from being a noble and warlike knight . . .

> He had in armes abroad wonne muchell fame. . . .*

This unusual kinship of man with animal is emphasised again in the origin of humanity or, at least, of that part of it which Spenser calls "elfin kind" (to which several of his knights belong).†

* I. 6, 20 to 30.
† Spenser makes no very definite distinction between fairies and humans. Cf. Greenlaw, *Studies in Philology*, April 1918, p. 116 *seq.*

Prometheus composed his first man of parts of animals:

> Prometheus did create
> A man of many parts from beasts deryv'd
> And then stole fire from heven to animate
> His work . . .*

The transition from beast to man is, moreover, naturally accomplished through the savage, the "salvage man" who plays such a fine part in Cantos IV. and V. of Book VI.; there is certainly a little magic in him, since

> He was invulnerable made by magicke lore.

That is inevitable in *The Faërie Queene*, but in every other way he is a good representative of the primitive as Spenser imagines him: he knows no tongue and yet he is acquainted with the properties of herbs:

> For other language had he none nor speach
> But a soft murmur and confused sound
> Of senseless words, which nature did him teach....

He saves Calepine from the treachery and cruelty of Turpine, heals him, protects him, and then courteously accompanies Serena until their opportune meeting with Arthur. He knows no fear:

* II. 10, 70.

171

The salvage nation doth all dread despise,

and he harms nothing, but feeds on fruit:

> he fed on flesh, ne ever of wyld beast
> Did taste the bloud, obaying natures first beheast.

The lady he saved finally bestows on him this testimonial:

> In such a salvage wight of brutish kynd
> Among wilde beastes in desert forrests bred
> It is most straunge and wonderful to find
> So milde humanity and perfect gentle mynd.*

So Spenser's general sympathy with Nature† extends to those creatures she first produced, who remain in closest contact with her; and Spenser takes pleasure in discovering possible relationship between mankind and the lower animals. This is all the more interesting since it is less a matter of clearly formulated ideas than of poetically expressed feelings. Spenser delights in contact with nature, in the company of all "living wightes": to him nothing evil is necessarily associated with the lower forms of life, which "by kynde" do not differ essentially from humanity itself.

* VI. 4, 2 to 14; 5, 2 to 9, 29, etc.
† Nature has, however, an evil side which we will deal with later on.

He has, in addition to this, a very highly developed sense of nature's fruitfulness, a fruitfulness constantly associated with sensuality. Notice, first of all, that to Spenser sensuality (taking the word in its broadest meaning) is not in itself reprehensible. We need do no more than allude to that charming poem "Epithalamium," whose sensuality is so delicate and deeply felt, and note that here, as in the other nuptial poem, all nature is invited to, and takes part in, human marriage feasts. In *The Faërie Queene* the reunions of the knights with their ladies after trials and battles give opportunities for descriptions of a sensuality which is quite simple and innocent. The same feeling inspires "Epithalamium" and the description of Una's marriage.* It is no doubt as a contrast to this that the bestial sensuality which crops up so often in the narrative of *The Faërie Queene* is condemned as the height of abomination. Like his contemporaries, Spenser usually makes a distinction between love and lust without having to go into the matter at great length. The stanza at the beginning of Canto III. of Book III. shows this:

Most sacred fyre, that burnet mightily
In living brests ykindled first above
Emongst th' eternal sphers and lamping sky

* Cf. also the last stanzas of Book III. in the first edition, and V. 3, 40.

And thence poured into men, which men call love;
Not that same, which doth base affections move
In brutish minds, and filthy lust inflame
But that sweet fit that doth true beautie love.

For him, then, as for Milton later on, there exists
a legitimate and almost holy sensuality; a cosmic
element whence issues all life, which is not in
itself reprehensible either in man or in nature.
The full description of the female body arouses in
him feelings only of respect and admiration; there
is no need to quote the fine stanza in "Epithalamium." But a description lost at the end of Book
VI. is still more convincing:

Her ivorie neck, her alabaster brest,
Her paps, which like white silken pillows were,
For Love in soft delight thereon to rest;
Her tender sides, her bellie white and clere
Which like an altar did itself upreare
To offer sacrifice divine thereon;
Her goodly thighs, whose glory did appeare
Like a triumphall arch and there upon
The spoiles of princes hang'd which were in battle
     won;
Those daintie parts, the dearlings of delight
Which mote not be prophan'd of common eyes.*

So to Spenser there is nothing wrong in sensuality in itself, and we can approach the descrip-

* II. 8, 42-43.

tions of Nature's fruitfulness, knowing that her sensual character has no evil significance for him. It is true that he can speak to us on occasion, like the rest of his century, about "sinful mire" and "sinful flesh," but we may take these commonplaces as being not altogether representative of his own feelings.

The classical example, which we shall come across presently in the "Garden of Adonis," is that of the marriage of the Sun and the Earth, a marriage which is no metaphor but which is consummated by the penetration of the sun's fecundating rays into "earthes fruitful wombe," an idea handed down through the ages, very prevalent at the time of the Renaissance, and to be met with in England a quarter of a century or so later, after being scientifically developed by Fludd. Here it is, first of all, in pure rhetoric:

At last, the golden orientall gate
Of greatest heaven gan to open fayre;
And Phoebus fresh, as brydegrom to his mate,
Came dauncing forth, shaking his dewie hayre;
And hurld his glistring beams through gloomy ayre.

Phaedria's song in Canto VI. of Book II. gives us the motif taken up again later by Milton in *Comus:*

Wherefore did Nature pour her bounties fourth . . .

The two poets condemn the two characters that extol nature's call, but both poets feel and echo this call in an equally moving way:

Behold, o man, that toilsome paines doest take,
The flowrs, the fields and all that pleasaunt
　　growes,
How they themselves doe thine ensample make
Whiles nothing envious nature them forth throwes
Out of her fruitfull lap: how, no man knowes
They spring, they bud, they blossom fresh and
　　faire
And decke the world with their rich pompous
　　showes. . . .

We have here the bases of a purely materialistic conception of nature (that is why Spenser puts it into the mouth of a condemned person; this procedure common at the time of the Renaissance must not throw us off the scent):

. . . how, no man knowes . . .

Milton's Satan, bolder still, goes further:

This fair Earth I see
Warmed by the Sun, producing every kind
Them (the gods) nothing.*

* *Par. Lost*, ix. 719.

176

Phaedria continues:

> The lilly, lady of the flowering field
> The flowre de luce, her lovely paramoure,
> Bid thee to them thy fruitless labors yield . . .
> What boots it all to have and nothing use?*

And this Nature who incites men to follow her example is none other than Venus herself. The hymn to Venus in Book IV. explains this clearly:

> . . . the daedale earth throw forth to thee (Venus)
> Out of her fruitful lap aboundant flowers;
> And then all living wights, soone as they see
> The spring breake forth out of his lusty covers,
> They all doe learn to play the paramours:
> First doe the merry birds, thy prety pages
> Privily pricked with thy lustful powers
> Chirpe loud to thee out of their leavy cages
> And thee their mother call to coole their kindly rages,
> In generation seek to quench their inward fire.
> So all the world by thee at first was made
> And dayly yet thou doest the same repayre . . .†

This fruitfulness is also to be noted in the sea:

> O what an endless worke have I in hand,
> To count the seas abundant progeny!
> So fertile be the flouds in generation
> So huge their numbers, and so numberless their
>    nation.

* *F.Q.*, II. 6, 15 to 17.   † *F.Q.*, IV. 10, 44 to 47.

Here it is actually the "seas," the "flouds" which are the fruitful powers; Nature herself. Venus comes in as a merely rhetorical figure; for it is certainly of the fruitfulness of the Earth that Spenser sings:

> Therefore the antique wisards well invented
> That Venus of the fomy sea was bred.*

But it is easy to discern an element of fear in Spenser's feelings in the face of all this extraordinary creative power. Apart even from her fruitfulness, there is in Nature something evil. Awesome scenes are frequent in *The Faërie Queene*. Here is one example:

> Where that same wicked wight
> His dwelling has, low in an hollow cave
> Far underneath a craggy cliff ypight
> Dark, dolefull, dreary, like a greedy grave
> On top wherof ay dwelt the ghastly owle,
> Shrieking his baleful note. . . .†

And here is a second:

> Under a steep hilles side it placed was
> And fast beside a little brooke did pass
> Of muddie water, that like puddle stanke
> By which few crooked sallowes grew in ranke.‡

* *F.Q.*, IV. 12, 1 and 2. † *F.Q.*, I. 9, 33. ‡ *F.Q.*, IV. 5, 33.

The forest we saw in smiling mood now frowns:

They come unto a forrest greene
In which they shrowd themselves . . .
Yet feare them follows still, where so they beene:
Each trembling leafe and whistling wind they
    heare
As ghastly bug, does greatly them affeare. . . .*

Fear has followed these personages, but the
details of the description are exact. The sea naturally has its dangers also.† But two things above
all others trouble the poet: the rapid changes in
Nature; and, in her very fruitfulness, the multipli-
cation of monsters and evil beings.

In nature's incitement to voluptuousness there
is a sinister side. Spenser takes up the theme,
Gather ye roses while ye may, with a very personal
feeling: It is because beauty quickly fades that
we must hasten to enjoy it; and we must do the
same with life:

Ah see the virgin rose, how sweetly shee
Doth first peep forth with bashful modestee
. . . Lo see soone after how more bold and free
Her bared bosome she doth broad display
Lo see soone after how she fades and falls away
So passeth, in the passing of a day

* *F.Q.*, II. 3, 20.    † Cf. II. 2, 24; IV. 1, 42, etc.

Of mortal life the leafe, the bud, the flowre
Ne more doth florish after first decay
. . . Gather therfore the rose while yet is prime.*

And in nature's fruitfulness, also, there is danger:

Most ugly shapes and horrible aspects
Such as dame Nature selfe mote feare to see,
Or shame, that ever should so fowle defects
From her most cunning hand escaped bee;
All dreadfull pourtraicts of deformitee. . . .†

Then follows a list of sea monsters:

For all that here on earth we dreadfull hold
Be but as bugs to fearen babes withall,
Compared to the creatures in the seas entrall.

The poet is also eloquent on the multitude of ill-omened birds:

Such as by nature men abhor and hate.‡

And if satyrs and savages are at times worthy of esteem, wicked satyrs and cannibals do exist as well:

* *F.Q.*, II. 12, 23 and 25.    † II. 12, 23 and 25.
‡ II. 12, 36.

Thereto they used one most accursed order
To eat the flesh of men . . .
A monstrous cruelty gainst course of kynde!*

This is because Nature, which seems to have
been kindly and well ordered in the beginning,
is in process of deterioration. She appears to be
returning to final chaos, having, as we shall see
in "The Garden of Adonis," issued from primitive chaos. We read in Spenser's translation of
du Bellay's *Ruins of Rome*:

Ye cruel stars and else ye gods unkind
Heaven envious and bitter stepdame Nature!
I say not as the common voyce doth say
That all things which beneath the moon have
    being
Are temporal. . . .
But I say rather,
That all this whole shall one day come to nought!

and also (XXII.):

So when the compass of this Universe
In six and thirty thousand years is ronne,
The bands of the elements shall back reverse
To their first discord, and be quite undone.
The seeds of which all things at first were bred
Shall in great Chaos wombe again be hid.

* VI. 8, 36.

In *The Faërie Queene* Spenser explains to us that the whole world is leaving its old ways and departing from its original magnificent plan. And rather forgetting that he is a Christian, Spenser gives no orthodox reason for this grievous event. He does not tell us, as Milton does later on, that it is man's fault that nature is disorganised and that the fall of Adam is the cause of the cosmic catastrophe. On the contrary, Spenser seems to insist on the fact that man became evil because he was involved in the general deterioration of the whole of nature: he laments the decadence of nations:

For that which all men then did virtue call
Is now cald vice . . .
Right is now wrong, and wrong that was is right;
As all things else in time are chaunged quight.

And he adds that this is not surprising:

No wonder; for the heavens revolution
Is wandred farre from where it first was pight,
And so doe make contrarie constitution
Of all this lower world toward his dissolution.*

The poet sees proofs of this progress of nature towards ultimate chaos in astronomy:

* *F.Q.*, V., introduction, 4 to 8.

For whoso list into the heavens looke
And search the courses of the rowling spheares
Shall find that from the point where first they tooke
Their setting forth, in these few thousand years,
They all are wandred much . . .

And he gives us exact details of the changes in
the position of the stars right from ancient times.
He returns to this same subject in the "Mutability
Cantos":

That even these Stargazers stonisht are
At sight thereof, and damne their lying bookes.*

We find thus, in the poem as a whole, a fairly wide
basis for the two fragments, "The Garden of
Adonis" and the "Mutability Cantos," which are
more properly philosophical. Throughout the
whole of *The Faërie Queene* nature is alive; nature
is fruitful and sensual; nature is changeable and
corruptible.

Taking these feelings and ideas as a basis, we
find rather more complicated, though hardly more
definite, conceptions of Nature's fruitfulness in
"The Garden of Adonis"; and of her corruptibility
in the "Mutability Cantos." In the first poem a
sort of nature pantheism is expressed, but the
frailty of living beings is equally emphasised; in
the second fragment, it is the latter idea which is

* "M.C.," VIII. 52.

mainly developed, but the conception of nature as supreme is also to be found.

In my opinion, one must at all costs avoid classifying Spenser's ideas. He rarely makes use of ideas expressed in one part of his poem in another. The "Mutability Cantos" start quite a new semi-philosophical *exposé* which has nothing whatever to do with what was said in "The Garden of Adonis." Consequently, it seems to me that it is necessary to study separately the content of each one of these pieces.

## 3. THE GARDEN OF ADONIS

Let us note first of all the extremely episodic character of this piece. It is in Canto VI. of Book III. that the poet initiates us, quite by chance as it seems, into his most important philosophical conceptions. Might this mean that he does not himself take them very seriously? Wishing to give his chaste heroine, Belphoebe, a chaste birth, he imagines for her an immaculate conception:

Pure and unspotted from all loathly crime
That is ungenerate in fleshly slime.

Too much importance must not be attached to this sudden harking back to Christianity, since the poet at the same time causes Amoretta, who is destined to be the pattern of lady-loves, to be born in the same circumstances. And, in reality, the sexual character of the creation of the twins is not the less marked for being cosmic.

It is the sun who is the father of the twins, he having sent his rays into the body of their mother:

> Being through former bathing mollified,
> And pierst into her womb.

And here is the poet explaining that after all the sun is the universal father as the earth is the universal mother:

> Great father he of generation
> Is rightly called, th'authour of life and light;
> And his fair sister for creation
> Ministreth matter fit, which tempred right
> With heat and humour breedes the living wight.

This ancient pagan idea, that the Renaissance took very seriously, is expressed in another episode forming a preface to "The Garden of Adonis"; though it is not connected in any way with the conception of the garden itself. There we come across the sexual element again, but this time it is Venus and Adonis who play the rôle of the Earth and the Sun.

The Garden of Adonis seems to me to be a symbol of the generation of the natural species.

Developing poetically, but somewhat vaguely, conceptions already expressed elsewhere in *The Faërie Queene*, the poet depicts the procreative power of Nature:

> There is the first seminary
> Of all things that are borne to live and dye
> According to their kynds.

But this symbol or allegory is not carried to its utmost limit, and several rather ill-assorted elements, from the point of view of philosophy, follow one another in the description. This is another proof that Spenser did not attach great importance to the expression of definite ideas but was content to convey poetically feelings of wonder and astonishment at the fruitfulness of nature.

First of all, he puts before us an extremely rudimentary theory of reincarnation; Old Genius, who stands for nothing in particular, is the gate-keeper of this garden:

> A thousand thousand naked babes attend
> About him day and night, which do require
> That he with fleshly weeds would them attire.
> Such as him list, such as eternal fate
> Ordained hath, he clothes with sinful mire.

Note his vagueness when he resumes:

> Such as him list, such as eternal fate
> Ordained hath.

The poet seems to correct himself, to substitute, for the high-handedness of Genius, eternal fate, without taking the trouble to erase "such as him list," which remains to contradict the words that follow. For to make the will of Genius equivalent to eternal fate would be to give this personage an importance out of all reason. Besides, there is no further mention of him or of this "eternal fate."

Men (here it is a question of "naked babes" clothed with "sinful mire," therefore human beings) are in this way brought into the world, and, when they die, they go back into the garden and remain there "some thousand yeares":

And grow afresh—
And then of him are clad with other hew,
Or sent into the changeful world againe
Till thether they returne, where first they grew;
So like a wheele arownd they runne from old to new.

This conception of reincarnation is remarkable for its lack of morality. Plato had carefully pointed out that these returns to the world of the living are made according to rules governing the retribution of vice and virtue. There is nothing of that sort here. It is strange that, in a poem so moral in intention as *The Faërie Queene*, Spenser should miss this opportunity of improving us. And this lends force to M. Legouis' assertion* that the

* Spenser, p. 98.

"moralities" in *The Faërie Queene* are extraneous, and that what interests Spenser is the story he is relating. Here in the same way it is the idea of reincarnation which interests him and not its moral significance. No doubt he sees in it one aspect of this mutability of nature which makes such an impression on him. Moreover, the idea of fruitfulness makes him forget this conception of returns. He maintains that beings grow of themselves:

> Ne needs there gardiner to sett or sow
> To plant, or prune, for of their owne accord
> All things as they created were do grow . . .
> For in themselves eternall moisture they imply.

Then the poet's thought changes; he loses sight of men, he forgets his theory of reincarnation, of the return of these same beings to the garden; he explains to us, on the contrary, that an infinite number of creatures can be sent from this garden on to the earth without ever diminishing the stock, because creative chaos is continually filling the garden. Now this is true also of men, for of these forms growing there, there are

> Some fit for reasonable sowles to endue (35).

The poet is no longer troubled about the theory set out three stanzas before, for there it was the souls who were waiting in the garden to be "clothed

with sinful mire." These are now forms, that is to
say bodies:

Infinite shapes of creatures there are bred,
And uncouth forms . . .
Some made for beasts, some made for birds to
      weare,
And all the fruitful spawn of fishes hew.

For the poet does not differentiate between the
animals and the "reasonable souls," all inter-
mingling in one and the same stanza.

It seems to me, then, that between one stanza
(33) and another (35) the drift of the poet's thought
has changed; what now occupies his mind is
nature's infinite fruitfulness; it is impossible to reconcile the similar expression of two different ideas.

Daily they grow, and daily forth are sent
Into the world—
Yet is the stock not lessened nor spent.

We pass now to a third idea, which has no logical
connection, either, with the foregoing ideas. The
substance from which all beings are derived is in
a perpetual chaos; one moment they come out of
it, the next they fall back into it:

For in the wide wombe of the world there lyes
In hateful darkness and in deep horrore
An huge eternall chaos, which supplyes
The substance of natures fruitful progenyes.

All things from thence doe their first being fetch,
And borrow matter, wherof they are made,
Which, whenas forme and feature it does ketch,
Becomes a body and doth then invade
The state of life out of the greesly shade.
That substance is eterne and bideth so
Ne when the life decayes and forme does fade,
Doth it consume and into nothing goe
But changed is—
For every substance is conditioned
To change her hew, and sondry forms to donne
        (36 to 38).

Now in stanza 33 it was the souls, on the contrary, who apparently were forms, who remained permanent and were

            clad with other hue.

And in 35 it was the bodies who were "forms." It cannot even be said that the poet is contradicting himself: he speaks of two different ideas, one after the other, without connecting them. Otherwise chaos would correspond to the garden, since the creatures issue from it at birth and return to it at death. Now, the garden is the very opposite of chaos, for in the garden everything is in perfect order (35)

        And ranckt in comely row.

It is not possible to establish a logical connection between these three ideas: the reincarnation of the same souls, the order of the different species in nature, and the chaos which supplies the substance of living beings. The poet passes from one to the other without linking them up with each other. And he goes on to a fourth idea which is still nearer to his heart—that of time, the destroyer of all things. Spenser is so far from giving us an orderly philosophical *exposé*, the lyrical element being so dominant in his poem, that he passes without any transition from the general idea

> For formes are variable, and decay
> By course of kind and by occasion

to the idea of the frailty of woman's beauty:

> And that faire flower of beautie fades away
> As doth the lily fresh before the sunny ray.

And that is what brings him to the idea of time:

> Great enemy to it, and to all the rest
> That in the garden of Adonis springs,
> Is wicked time. . . .

And while he is engaged with time and its ravages the poet forgets his distinction between substance and form. It is the beings themselves, no matter

191

what their constitution, that time destroys; and the garden is perpetually being destroyed by it. Note also that here the garden has passed into the phenomenal world where death prevails (39 and 40), while at the beginning, when Genius was presiding over it, the garden was not in the terrestrial world:

> Such as eternall fate
> Ordained hath, he cloths in sinful mire
> And sendeth forth to live in mortal state (32),

but in stanza 39,

> Wicked time, who with his scythe addrest
> Does mow the flowering herbes and goodly
>     things,

the poet's thought, lyrically inspired, has undergone one more change: he is altogether taken up with expressing the melancholy fact that

> All that lives is subject to that law,
> All things decay in time and to their end doe draw.

So that the garden, "the first seminary" (stanza 30), is transformed, on the contrary, into a place

> Where they do wither and are fowly mard.

This in spite of the gods, who, notwithstanding their pity, can do nothing in the matter.

And their great mother Venus did lament
The losse of her deare brood, her deare delight.

Then the feeling changes once more, and the poet, returning to his first symbol of generation, of love, describes the delights of love-making, opening with a singularly naive transition (41):

But were it not that time their trouble is,
All that in this delightful garden growes
Should happy be, and have immortal bliss.

All of which amounts to this, that if they were not mortal they would be immortal, and if they were not unhappy they would be happy. The preceding stanza describes Venus in tears and the garden laid waste; stanzas 41 and 42 the universal happiness of the beings in the garden. Philosophically, this is nonsense, but, poetically, the transition is permissible and the sequence of ideas clear: the love-making season is such a blissful one; what a pity it is so soon gone! Lyrical interpretation makes clear a passage which philosophical analysis could but destroy.

Running through the few stanzas coming before and after (40 to 48) we meet again, fully developed this time, the theme of the creation of things by the sexual act. We learned in stanza 40 that Venus is the mother of all things in the garden: "their great mother Venus," "her deare

brood." Stanza 46 describes the relations between
Venus and Adonis:

> And reap sweet pleasur of the wanton boy,
> —But she herself, whenever that she will,
> Possesseth him, and of his sweetness takes her
> fill.

And, in 47, Adonis is shown as being *"the father of
all forms," "that living gives to all."*

The theme presented at the beginning of the
canto in a "scientific" and cosmographic form—
that of the Sun-Earth union by which all things
are engendered—is here developed in a scheme
mythological. It was from the union of a male
deity and a female deity that all creatures, their
children, sprang. This is in harmony with some
features in *The Faërie Queene*, already pointed out;
and also with the introduction of Genius at the
beginning of this canto, the Genius that we met
with in Book II. (Canto XII., stanza 47).

> That celestial power to whom the care
> Of life, and generation of all
> That lives, perteines in charge particulare.

This general harmony of conception does not,
however, imply any connection, even a poetical
one, still less a logical one, between Genius on
the one hand and Venus and Adonis on the other.
Genius remains quite alone at the beginning of

the piece, opening and shutting the doors of the garden. Venus and Adonis are *inside* the garden, where the procreation apparently takes place: no need for doors or for Genius. This is another hiatus between the beginning and the end of the episode. But from stanza 43 the poet falls back into myth, and begins to put before us the Venus and Adonis idyll. He seems to have forgotten what went before, for he explains that Adonis lives in a grove,

> Whose shady boughes sharp steele did never lop
> Nor wicked beastes their tender buds did crop.

We could accept this anywhere else in *The Faërie Queene* where such retreats are not rare, but in the middle of this allegorical garden, where there is no enemy but time, these features should not have been brought in. There are in the garden neither "wicked beastes" nor "sharp steele."

> Ne needs there gardiner to sett or sow
> To plant or prune,

he told us in stanza 39. If there is so little coherence in the description, we must not expect to find it in the ideas either.

One more stanza plunges us again into philosophy and contradictions; it concerns Adonis (17):

> For he may not
> For ever dye and ever buried bee
> In baleful night where all things are forgot;

All he be subject to mortalitie,
Yet is eterne in mutabilitie
And by succession made perpetuall,
Transformed oft, and changed diverslie
For him the father of all forms they call;
Therefore needs mote he live that living gives
    to all.

Mr. Greenlaw, who has laboured more than any other man in the world to put this garden of Adonis in order, tries to see in Adonis substance and in Venus form.* The two lines

Subject to mortalitie,
Yet eterne in mutabilitie

seem indeed to apply to the substance described in stanza 37:

That substance is eterne and bideth so
Ne when the life decayes and form does fade
Does it consume and into nothing go,
But changed is and often altred to and fro.

But if Adonis is substance, what is the meaning of this line?

For him the father of all forms they call.

And, moreover, no indication is apparent in this passage that Venus is form. Generally it is the male element which is supposed to represent form and the female element substance. Thus at the be-

* *Studies in Philology*, July 1920, p. 332.

SPENSER'S PHILOSOPHICAL IDEAS

ginning of the canto we saw the Sun, male, shape
the substance provided by the Earth, his sister, who

Ministreth matter fit (9).

My belief is simply that the poet is not referring
to a previously expressed idea of opposition between matter and form. The drift of the poem
has changed again; Adonis now represents Being,
living beings, the whole of nature: he is both substance and form, continually being transformed
and never dying. Venus has no philosophical rôle in
this part of the myth. Adonis alone has a meaning.

As to the wild boar, Adonis's enemy (stanza 48),
fast shut in under the hill, Mr. Greenlaw sees in
him chaos* which will one day destroy the world.
I find no foundation in the poem for such an
interpretation. If Adonis is substance (as in Mr.
Greenlaw's hypothesis) the boar cannot be his
enemy, since substance is never destroyed but
only form. The wild boar should therefore be the
enemy of Venus. Moreover it is said (36) that chaos

supplies
The substance of nature's fruitfull progenyes.

This in the myth would necessitate the boar who
kills Adonis (substance) being the father of Adonis,
which is, of course, absurd.

* *Studies in Philology*, July 1920, pp. 332, 333. If one must
allegorise the boar it would be better to make it stand for
*Time*, who is represented as being the enemy of the "forms"
in the garden. But even that has no philosophical meaning. To
Spenser, Time was certainly not fettered or rendered harmless.

197

My belief is that the boar has no philosophical rôle, that Spenser is simply going on with his story of Venus and Adonis, and that by stanza 48 he has finished with the philosophical part. For what does this Adonis stand for now?

There now he liveth in eternal bliss.

No philosophical idea can now be associated with Adonis's happiness if he is substance undergoing continual change. Often, in *The Faërie Queene*, Spenser forgets his allegory and puts into his narrative many interesting but inexplicable details. He does the same with philosophy.

To sum up: philosophical analysis shows us in "The Garden of Adonis" a sequence of six ideas, frequently at variance with each other: the re-incarnation of the same souls (32-33); the fruit-fulness of Nature in her different species (34-35); chaos-substance and the transitoriness of form (36-38); time the great destroyer (39-40); the beauty of the love-making season (41-42); the immortality of being throughout its changes. No logical connection runs through the development or the sequence of the ideas, and we saw in the detailed analysis that the poet is quite indifferent to contradictions. The fact is that, in reality, philosophy does not come in here. We have before us a piece which is, in the main, lyrical. The poet wishes to express his feeling about nature's fruit-fulness, a fruitfulness connected with the changes of nature; this marvellous fruitfulness is only the everlasting change of one and the same substance. So, leaving on one side the logical exposition, we see very clearly the train of feelings in the poetical expression; and the whole of this canto, absurd if looked upon as philosophy, is very beautiful and rich in sensual impressions and in philosophical "sentiment" if looked upon as poetry.

The poet sees Nature first of all as a great storehouse of seed. What interests him most are human souls, which consequently he causes to move in cycles; he is struck by the idea of change in her seeds or forms, and does not bother about morality (32-33); then the fruitfulness of non-human nature occurs to him, as a natural corollary of the preceding idea (34-35); going further down the scale, below man and animal, he arrives at chaos, and sees in it the eternal substance of the world (36-38). This, by inevitable contrast, reminds him sharply of the infinite changes in the form of this substance, of the beauty of these forms, and the cruelty of time which destroys them (39-40), but he consoles himself with the old reflection of the poets that, if beauty is short-lived, it is nevertheless fair while it lasts. "Gather ye roses . . ." Hence his description of beauty and love (41-42). In conclusion, he essays in a final stanza a general summing up.

It is waste of time to look in all this for Aristotle's substance and form; substance is not defined at all, it is hardly differentiated from form; there are not here even the beginnings of a philosophical statement.

But there are here feelings which are at the base of all philosophy, feelings whose expression is highly poetic at times, and always, by its constant changes, alluring, mysterious and moving. And there is the very deep feeling that nature is an animate thing, fruitful, sensual and, unhappily for our feelings, eternally changing. And also the deep-rooted feeling that all beings are made of the same plastic matter, living and infinitely transformable; this is the pantheism of the poets, who feel Nature too keenly, who rejoice too much in her life and grieve too deeply over her changes:

> To see so faire things mard and spoiled quight;
> And their great mother Venus did lament
> The loose of her deare brood, her dear delight
> Her heart was pierst with pity at the sight.

It is this last impression, that of the constant change in nature, that we shall find again in the "Mutability Cantos."

## 4. THE "MUTABILITY CANTOS"

If "The Garden of Adonis" is an episode, the two cantos on Mutability are a separate fragment, whose connection with *The Faërie Queene* has even been questioned.* The last passage in the frag-

* Cf. the bibliography on this point in Carpenter: *Reference Guide to Spenser*, p. 165.

ment does indeed contain an appeal to the almighty God of the Christians, which is hardly in keeping with the great pagan poem.

On the other hand, it would seem that the "Mutability Cantos" contain more important ideas in Spenser's eyes than does "The Garden of Adonis." First of all, the fragment stands by itself; it is not an episode introduced to bring in outside events or personages. It has no connection whatever with the rest of *The Faërie Queene*. Then, it takes up a subject to which Spenser has already given a place of honour and which he has treated at length in the introduction of Book V., showing that he had this idea at heart. Finally, the idea is this time developed in an ordered manner. These two cantos take up another theme we have already encountered. It is the old Christian idea' that there are two orders of things: the earthly order where change prevails, and the heavenly order where all things are perfect and changeless. Let me quote once again the "Ruins of Rome":

. . . I say not as the common voyce doth say
That all things which beneath the moon have
    being
Are temporal . . .
But I say rather
That all this Whole shall one day come to nought.

Was that Spenser's idea? And as Milton was on

the side of the devil, was Spenser on the side
of Mutability? The subject of Canto VI. is set
forth in the same terms as that of "The Ruins of
Rome":

> Proud change (not pleased in mortal things
> Beneath the moone to raigne)
> Pretends as well of gods as men
> To be the soveraine.

Here Spenser says "as the common voyce doth
say" that *change* is wrong. But does he think it?
He speaks *as the common voice* does for three
stanzas; and as du Bellay for two cantos. He is
evidently much more alive to the arguments of
Mutability than to those of the opposite camp.
Now it is the whole of religion which is at stake:
if Mutability is right, if she rules in divine affairs
as in human affairs, religion is no longer possible.
Spenser's reason finds no case against Mutability.
So we see him take refuge—a very precarious
refuge, and a very temporary one—in religion.
Normally he is on the side of Mutability, no doubt
against the dictates of his feelings, and his feelings
make up for this in the religious passages which
have no logical connection with the rest of his
ideas.

Note here again that if nature has degenerated
it was not through the fault of man; it was Mutability who changed everything:

For she the face of earthly things so changed
That all which Nature had establisht first
In good estate, and in meet order ranged,
She did pervert, and all their statutes burst:
And all the world's fair frame (which none yet
    durst
Of Gods or men to alter or misguide)
She alter'd quite, and made them all accurst
That God had blest, and did at first provide
In that still happy state for ever to abide (VI. 5).

This is the second time Spenser explains the fall,
making it clear that it was not man's fault:

> . . . (which none yet durst
> Of Gods or men to alter or misguide).

Even death was introduced into the world by
Mutability and not by sin (VI. 6):

> O pittious work of Mutabilitie!
> By which we are all subject to that curse
> And death instead of life have sucked from our
>     nurse.

It is surely the Christian theme which is in Spenser's
mind: inadvertently he forgets to speak only of
gods (of gods and men) and speaks of God:

> And made them all accurst
> That God had blest.

It was through Mutability's usurpation that death came, in defiance of justice:

> Ne shee the laws of Nature only brake
> But else of justice, and of policie,
> And wrong of right and bad of good did make,
> And death for life exchanged foolishlie
> Since which all living wights have learnt to die
> And all this world is waxen daily worse (VI. 6).

Note the absence of all contradiction, of all indecision on this point. Spenser, who showed himself so fickle in his ideas in "The Garden of Adonis," is here quite sure of himself; he repeats twice over, here and in the introduction to Book V., the same conceptions. And he speaks for himself and not, as in the arguments which now follow, in the name of condemned Mutability. Let us bear in mind, then, the ideas expressed in this beginning so that what is to come may be more clear.

The only idea of Spenser which may be termed cosmogonic is his conception of Chaos, an ever-moving substance, from which all come forth and to which all return; we found it in "The Garden of Adonis," where it was the only logical idea. In this conception change is the very essence of things: Spenser conveys this mythologically, by making Mutability the daughter of Earth, herself the daughter of Chaos (VI. 26).

I am a daughter
Of her that is grand mother magnifide
Of all the gods, great Earth, great Chaos child.

And the first impression of the gods when
Mutability revolts is that Chaos has come back
(VI. 14).

Fearing lest Chaos broken had his chaine
And brought on them again eternal night.

Now this conception of chaos-substance can hardly
be called an idea in Spenser. It is the barely
intellectualised transposition of his deep feeling
of the vicissitudes of the world, of the natural
world as well as of the human world. This is the
very form which his sensibility, his perception of
nature and life take. He cannot rid himself of it;
that is why his religious ideas are no more than
passing outbursts of faith. When his outlook on
the world becomes unbearable, despair makes
him turn, as a last resort, to religion.

And is there care in heaven? and is there love
In heavenly spirits to these creatures bace
That may compassion of their evils move?
There is: else much more wretched were the cace
Of men than beasts.*

*F.Q., II. 8, 1.

But his normal view of the world as a thing of change is in its essence irreligious. Religion adopted under pressure of feeling comes to him from without, is not arrived at by his intelligence. Mutability, condemned by the gods, makes an appeal (VI. 36):

> But to the highest him, that is behight
> Father of gods and men by equall might,
> To weet the god of nature, I appeale.

Nature, the sovereign power, is above the gods. This is the highest pantheistic conception to which Spenser rises. Now a purely negative conception like that of chaos-substance is as repugnant to feeling as to intelligence. In this chaos-substance there is an element making for order, organisation, law; it may be constantly defeated (Spenser obviously knows nothing about that, but he greatly fears it), but it is constantly acting. This positive power, which is at work in Chaos, is Nature:

> An huge eternall Chaos, which supplyes—
> The substance of *natures* fruitfull progenyes.*

That is almost all Spenser knows about this "Nature." So he remains as indefinite as possible when describing her. She is veiled, no one knows

* *F.Q.*, III. 6, 36.

whether she is male or female; she is beyond
human understanding, and in the end she disappears "whither no man wist":

Yet certes by her face and physnomy
Whether she man or woman inly were
That could not any creature well descry;
For with a veil that wimpled everywhere
Her head and face was hid, that mote to none
    appeare (VII. 5).

She is the universal mother, and in her irreconcilables are reconciled:

This great grand mother of all creatures bred
Great Nature, ever yong, yet full of eld
Still moving, yet unmoved from her sted,
Unseene of any, yet of all beheld (VII. 13).

This corresponds in some way to the neo-platonists' complete indetermination of the supreme
Essence, interpreted however in terms of the
Renaissance, when theories of immanence were
beginning to take the place of those of transcend-
ence. The supreme Indeterminate was placed
neither beyond the world nor above it but in the
world itself. So, taking care not to be too definite,
Spenser makes use here of a conception prevalent
in his day. I have pointed out that he was led into
doing this by his own view of things, and so it was

with most of the minds of his age; the passionate interest then taken in external nature and the progress of budding science dominated the majority of thinkers. So the supposed existence of a vague general connection between Spenser and Giordano Bruno arises from the intellectual atmosphere of the sixteenth century.*

Examined more closely, this *Nature*, reconciler of all irreconcilables, can offer no satisfactory solution to the problems raised by Mutability. Obviously Nature's very function is to reconcile change and order since she herself is

Still moving, yet unmoved from her sted.

But this answer, borrowed from a philosophy of the Absolute, does not solve the problems which are raised in a philosophy of Nature. Chaos-substance, too, remains substantially the same throughout all its variations. This theoretical conception does not satisfy Spenser. In this vague pantheism, for instance, the immortality and the mortality of the soul are equally admissible: our whole being, perhaps, is taken back into the total substance and melted down into other forms. We see that this is one of the things which trouble the poet; and the idea that other beings will be formed from him does not console him for his own dis-

* Cf. Greenlaw, *Stud. in Phil.*, July 1920, p. 340; and against, S. B. Liljegren, *Rev. Lit. Comp.*, 1923, No. 4.

appearance. The required solution Nature cannot give, for she has to reconcile irreconcilables; and reason and human feelings are never satisfied by this. Therefore, as a last resort, the poet turns to religion: in it irreconcilables are not reconciled, but the survival of the soul and the justice of God are clearly and resolutely affirmed.

Let us now examine the development of Mutability's arguments. We find here the poet's own thought:

For heaven and earth I both alike do deeme
Sith heaven and earth are both alike to thee (VII.),

says Mutability to Nature. The reconciliation of opposites serves just as well to justify change in the divine order of things as order in human change. Nature cannot therefore give a decision and Mutability marks this from the start. Scepticism, then, notes the death of all existing things; the earth is ever changing (VII. 18).

For all that from her springs, and is ybredde,
However fair it flourish for a time
Yet see we soone decay; and being dead
To turne again unto their earthly slime;
Yet out of their decay and mortall crime
We daily see new creatures to arise.

It is really the question of personal immortality which occupies the poet's mind: if he could be sure of the survival of the soul, disorder would disappear. The following stanza applies the general rule directly to man (19):

> As for her tenants, that is man and beasts;
> The beasts we daily see massacred dy . . .
> And men themselves do change continually . . .
> Ne do their bodies only flit and fly
> But eeke their minds (which they immortall call)
> Still change and vary thoughts, as new occasions
>    fall.

Then Mutability turns to the elements and applies the law to them:

> Ne is the water in more constant case (20).

Two things are to be noted: first of all, in the order of the description man is placed between beasts that die and elements that pass away. He is but an item in the list of those who perish; he is not privileged in any way. Secondly, Mutability's argument is broken off: the conclusion *then man wholly dies* is not given. But we have this which is pure raillery:

> But eeke their minds (which they immortall call).

Professor Greenlaw* points out the analogy be-

* *Studies in Philology*, Oct. 1920, p. 460.

tween this argument and that of Lucretius, all
things change, all things die; man changes, man
dies. Now, since Mutability is to be officially
condemned at the end of the canto, why did not
Spenser dare to put the whole of the argument
into her mouth?

Because he finds it goes too deep; because he
knows he has nothing but a general idea, expressed
in one short stanza, with which to refute it; because he has no argument with which to counter
it; and because he does not wish to be accused of
atheism. He is therefore content to state the pre-
mises without coming to any conclusion (other
than "which they immortall call"), because the
conclusion is irrefutable by his intelligence.

Then Mutability describes the changes in the
elements, in each one, and from one to the other.

Yet they are chang'd by other wondrous slights
Into themselves and lose their native mights;
The fire to air, and the ayre to water sheere
And water into earth, yet water fights
With fire, and aire with earth approaching neare . . .
So in them all raignes mutabilite.

Then comes the procession of seasons, months,
hours, life and death; let us single out in passing
this remark on Death, which savours greatly of
paganism:

Yet is he naught but parting of the breath (46),

an altogether materialistic explanation on which
the poet does not lay much stress. Then, going
on with the statement of her case, Mutability
attacks the gods. She had already noticed that
these had no power over the elements, no matter
what they said.

For who sees not that time on all doth pray,
—So nothing here standeth in one stay,

she now concludes (47).
   Jupiter replies in one stanza (48), and it is to
be noted that his answer, which will be refuted,
is substantially the answer Nature gives (58).
The gods rule over time and the changes in things,
says Jupiter:

— is it not namely wee
Which poure that vertue from our heavenly all
That moves them all, and makes them changed be?
So them we gods doe rule. . . .

Nature says (58):

Then over them change doth not rule and raigne
But they raigne over change, and do their states
      maintaine.

Mutability's answer applies therefore to the final
judgment, after which Spenser can allow her to

speak no more. And this reply is pure scepticism—
one can go further, even pure science* (49).

>The things
>Which we see not how they are moved and swayed,
>Ye may attribute to yourselves as kings
>And say they by your secret powers are made:
>But what we see not, who shall us perswade?

This negatives Nature's final reply, as well as
Jupiter's argument. Mutability, then, shows that
the gods themselves change: their stars cannot
keep in their course. Spenser diverts the argument
on to scientific ground. The purely rhetorical
question of the changes in the pagan gods does
not interest him. The question of the disturbances
of the heavenly bodies is, on the contrary, important: astrology was a very living thing in the
sixteenth century, and it was important to prove
that order did not reign even in the starry spheres.
There was thus a connection between the wander-
ings of the planets and the vicissitudes of the
things of this world; and whether one believed in
astrology or not, in either case the theory that the
world was governed by a divine power was imperilled. Now here it is certainly Spenser who is
speaking and not Mutability, for we came across

* Mr. Greenlaw has noted that Spenser was not unac-
quainted with the scientific thought of his time. *Studies in
Philology*, April 1923, p. 242; Oct. 1920, p. 464.

the same arguments at the beginning of Book V. Having thus stated her case, Mutability awaits the verdict with confidence:

> Silence long ensewed
> Ne Nature to or fro spake for a space.

Spenser makes Nature hesitate. Is it for rhetorical effect? To convey to us the anxious suspense of those present? Not altogether. It is also because Nature does not know how to reply; what she has to say, what she ought to say, has already been refuted. Her answer takes up only one stanza, 58, and the contrast between her reply, a brief and simple affirmation, and the long logical unfolding of Mutability's arguments is noteworthy:

> I well consider all that ye have sayd
> And find that all things stedfastnes doe hate
> And changed be; yet being rightly wayd,
> They are not changed from their first estate;
> But by their change their being do dilate;
> And turning to themselves at length againe
> Do worke their owne perfection so by fate.
> Then over them change doth not rule and raigne
> But they raigne over change and do their states maintaine.

> Cease therefore daughter, further to aspire
> And thee content thus to be rul'd by me

For thy decay thou seekest by thy desire
But time shall come that all shall changed be
And from thenceforth none no more change shall
    see.

This is supposed to confirm Jupiter's rights. In
reality, it does nothing of the sort. Nature says:

And thee content thus to be rul'd by me.

It is she who rules, not the gods. Then she disappears:

Then was that whole assembly quite dismist
And Natures self did vanish, whither no man wist.

Nature therefore leaves things as they were. Mutability will continue her ravages, under the nominal
though not actual rule of the gods. It is Nature
who rules. In the first part of her answer she
transferred to the beings themselves the power
to rule over time, which the gods claimed: things
"raigne over change":

But by their change their being do dilate
—do work their own perfection.

To this Mutability has already replied, first of all:

But what we see not, who shall us perswade?

Then she put forth her argument against the gods: they themselves change, they are therefore subject to time and not the masters of time, an argument applying at least as much to "things" as to the gods. The idea of final perfection to which all things shall at last come has already been sneered at by Mutability when she told the gods (5-4):

> Then ye are mortall borne, and thrall to me
> Unless the kingdom of the skye yee make
> Immortal and unchangeable to be.

Then, to Spenser speaking through the mouth of Nature (which is always questionable as an expression of the author's own thought) we can oppose Spenser himself, speaking at the beginning of Book V. Things are not moving towards perfection but towards destruction; perfection existed at the beginning of the world:

> for the heavens revolution
> Is wandred far from where it first was pight
> And so doe make contrarie constitution
> Of all this lower world toward his dissolution.*

But (having agreed that one passage of Spenser is a very uncertain clue to the meaning of another passage some way off) let us turn back to the beginning of the "Mutability Cantos" (VI. 5):

* *F.Q.*, V. 4.

All the worlds faire frame . . . (Mutabilitie)
She alter'd quite, and made them all accurst
That God had blest, and did at first provide
In that still happy state for ever to abide.

In this Spenser finds a solution. But this solution is at variance with his own "philosophy." Beings were perfect in the beginning, at the time of their creation by a perfect creator. His philosophy told him that in the beginning they had come out of chaos and that they would return to it. A supreme effort of thought makes him put forward the extreme hypothesis that instead of returning to chaos they will return to perfection. But he has no reason to believe it, and he does not in any way expand the idea, which is refuted by his whole view of things. Therefore he abandons his philosophy and turns to his religion. God created things perfect; God will know how to give them back their perfection. Nature, by herself, is powerless. Hence the two stanzas in Canto VIII., in which the appeal rises, direct and powerful, to God:

Thenceforth all shall rest eternally
With him that is the God of Sabbaoth bright,
O that great Sabbaoth God, grant me that Sabbaoth sight.

It is this solution that Spenser tried to put in Nature's mouth in the reply in stanza 58 (VII.)

but it is not in keeping with Nature but only with
God. Spenser's reason does not supply him with
any arguments but those of the scepticism of his
day. It is his religion which gives him the solution
he desires. Things, left to themselves, move towards destruction. Nature herself said:

Doe worke their own perfection so by fate.

What is this *fate* which intervenes at the last
moment to save all things? Philosophy has no
answer. Religion has: it is God.

## 5. RELIGIOUS FEELING IN SPENSER

Religion was therefore necessary to Spenser—
it was necessary to his nature, and yet impossible
to his mind. Hence his sudden changes; hence
in the "Mutability Cantos" two Christian stanzas
following two pagan cantos; hence two Christian
hymns following two pagan hymns; two Christian hymns written about the time he finished
the six cantos of the great pagan poem. Hence in
the middle of *The Faërie Queene* this impulse
towards the divine love which alone renders the
world endurable:

And is there care in heaven? and is there love
In heavenly spirits to these creatures bace

That may compassion of their evils move?
There is: else much more wretched were the cace
Of men than beasts: but o the exeeding grace
Of highest God! that loves his creatures so,
And all his works with merce doth embrace
That blessed angels he sends to and fro,
To serve to wicked man, to serve his wicked foe?...
... And all for love and nothing for reward
O why should hevenly God to men have such
    regard?

Because of his love. Hence the Hymne to Heavenly
Love and the Hymne to Heavenly Beautie. There
we have the Christian view of things: it was through
man's fall, through his wickedness that perfect
order was upset: it is through the love of God
that all will be put right. Not a trace of natural
philosophy, apparently, in the two last hymns.
So there are in Spenser two quite distinct groups
of ideas: God has no place in *The Faërie Queene*;
but the conception of nature is powerless to under-
mine the religion in the hymns. This contradiction
strikes us but it did not strike Spenser. First of all
we saw, by analysing "The Garden of Adonis,"
that his mind was little affected by contradictions.
Secondly, the whole of the Middle Ages and, after
them, a great part of the sixteenth century were
wont to make a distinction between the realm of
religion and the realm of science, not permitting
one to encroach upon the other. This was often

the last refuge of rationalist minds, who in this way ensured for themselves freedom to philosophise in peace. But more often still it arose from a deep-seated and perfectly sincere conviction of the impotence of reason to solve ultimate problems. Spenser had that kind of mind. We saw that he tried to make reason harmonise with his pessimistic knowledge of the world and the imperious needs of his sensibility. And we saw that he failed in this endeavour. These same needs of his sensibility

(else much more wretched were the cace of men
    than beasts)

inevitably led him to find in religion what his reason could not give him:

Many lewd layes (ah! woe is me the more!)
In praise of that mad fit which fooles call Love
I have in th' heat of youth made heretofore
That in light wits did loose affection move;
But all these follies now I do reprove
And turned have the tenor of my string
The heavenly prayers of true Love to sing.

Of course we must not take him altogether seriously; he does not entirely give up his secular interests; it is as much rhetorical as religious ardour which makes him speak of his "lewd layes." The fact remains, nevertheless, that the sentiment

expressed is, in the main, sincere, and it is repeated at the end of the last hymn:

Ah then, my hungry soul! which long hast fed
On idle fancies of thy foolish thought . . .
. . . Looke at last up to that Soveraine light.

These are no longer "lewd layes" composed "in
th' heat of youth"; these "idle fancies of thy foolish
thought" lasted a long time; this is his whole
sensual conception of things:

(And, with false beauties flattering faith misled
Hast after vain deceitfull shadowes sought.)

And, for the time, he repudiates all his pagan
thought. So he himself draws the line between
the two kingdoms, the kingdom of religion and
that of philosophy, a line which alone enables us
to introduce some sort of order into his philosophical conceptions as well as into his psychology
itself. It only remains for us to notice that his
religious poems or passages are short, rare and
fervent; the "lewd layes" and "fancies of foolish
thought," on the contrary, are spun out inter-
minably, and form the very substance of *The
Faërie Queene*. The normal condition of his soul
was paganism, sensual and more than half scep-
tical; religion came to him in irresistible but in-
frequent outbursts.

## II. SPENSER AND THE CABALA

Various hypotheses have been put forward to explain the enigmatical personage whom Spenser calls *Sapience*, to whom he devotes the second half of his fourth hymn, "An hymne of Heavenly Beautie." Charles C. Osgood, in a study entitled "Spenser's Sapience," published in *Studies in Philology*, April 1917, gathers together the results of various works published on this subject and concludes by showing that after all the problem is not yet properly solved. There are, indeed, obvious objections to all the suggested interpretations. It was first of all believed that she was the Idea of Beauty, found in Plato or rather in Ficino (Harrison, Winstanley), but this does not take into account the "personal" character that Spenser very clearly ascribes to *Sapience*. L. Winstanley, in her edition of the *Hymnes*, picks out points of resemblance between *Sapience* and the Virgin of the Catholic religion. But that is not at all in keeping with Spenser's "puritan" ideas, and many of the traits of *Sapience*, her creative power, for instance, cannot be ascribed to the Virgin Mary. J. B. Fletcher suggests that *Sapience* is the Holy Ghost (*Publications of the Modern Language Association of America*, t. xxvi., p. 452). But that is not in accordance with the very pronounced feminine character of *Sapience*.

Mr. Osgood finally makes a collection of passages in the Old Testament dealing with Wisdom (*Proverbs* viii. 30; *Wisdom* i. 6, 7; vii. 23, 24; ix. 4, 10; *Sirach*, xxiv. 3, 5), and finds in them various elements which, if elaborated, might have resulted in *Sapience*. But one can hardly imagine Spenser, who was certainly no theologian, devoting himself to these researches and this elaboration when he was not obliged to speak of Wisdom, and when, in the rest of his Hymns, he only made use of the commonplaces of the neo-platonists and the Christians of his day. Moreover, this elaboration of wisdom's characteristics was effected in Judaism, and culminated, in the Cabala particularly, in the constitution of a feminine Power, called the *Schekhina* or *Matrona*, closely allied to the Deity himself.

On a close examination of Spenser's *Sapience* we realise that all the characteristics of *Sapience* are to be found in the *Schekhina*. Hence the hypothesis that in his "Hymne of Heavenly Beautie" Spenser extols the *Matrona* of the cabalists.

From the Christian point of view, this is not unlikely. A whole school of Christian cabalists, with Pico della Mirandola and Reuchlin at the head of it, had adopted the Cabala, and at different periods the ecclesiastical authorities had actually encouraged this movement, hoping to find in it a means of converting the Jews to Christianity (they took it rather too much for granted that the Cabala expounded the dogma of the Trinity and proved the divinity of Christ). In England, in the following century, we find Robert Fludd (after 1617), Henry More and Milton interesting themselves in the Cabala. Now, the end of the sixteenth century perhaps marks the widest extension of cabalistic ideas. The two most famous commentaries of the *Zohar*, those of Louria and Corduero, belong to the middle of this century, and the *Zohar* was printed at Mantua and Cremona in 1559-1560.

In the present state of our knowledge it is hardly possible to know how Spenser could have had access to the Cabala. *A priori*, he could have read Reuchlin, Agrippa, Pico della Mirandola or some other cabalist of the fifteenth or sixteenth century; Giordano Bruno, who, in England, moved in circles frequented by Spenser's friends, could have made known the Cabala, which was familiar to him, to the poet's intellectual set. Obviously we cannot be certain about this. But it must be remembered that on a sensitive, enthusiastic and essentially literary mind a contemporary movement would have a much greater hold than a whole series of biblical passages. It seems to me much more credible that Spenser, at a certain period of his life, came under the influence of a mystical movement of his age than that he built up for himself, with the aid of the Old Testament, an intermediary power in connection with the

Deity. Spenser seems to have had nothing mystical about him. His nature seemed rather to incline him towards open sensuality and scepticism, but, as with many sixteenth-century temperaments, sudden fits of religiosity must have driven him, at times, to beliefs which were not normal to him. Now, among the more or less metaphysical entities in the Cabala, none was as likely as the Schekhina to attract and concentrate religious feeling. None other plays such a rôle or enjoys such popularity among cabalists. On the other hand, Wisdom in the Old Testament remains a colourless and debatable personage, with no very definite official place in dogma, sometimes identified with the Verb, sometimes with God himself, or considered as a mere attribute of God. She does not occupy a particularly important place in sixteenth-century Christian literature. Her presence in the Hymnes would seem a problem to be solved. But if, on the other hand, contact between Spenser and cabalistic ideas is admitted, then the rôle and importance of Wisdom, now the Schekhina, are quite clear.

Another thing in favour of our hypothesis is that it accepts as legitimate a good number of previous hypotheses, and that more particularly it is only the expansion of the well-thought-out ideas expressed by Osgood. The Bible texts which speak of wisdom form naturally the basis of the conception of the Schekhina, who is Wis-

dom. The Cabala speaks also on occasion of the
Holy Spirit, and as cabalists do not worry so
much as Christians about changes of sex, the
Holy Spirit of the *Zohar* could be considered as
being also the Schekhina, at least by anyone so
little initiated in these things as Spenser must
have been. We need not therefore reject Fletcher's
ideas either. Spenser may also have had in mind
Plato's Beauty (the Cabala certainly calls the Schekhina Beauty too*), and even the Virgin Mary
if so be that at one period of his life he inclined
towards Catholicism.† But these different influences only added to and strengthened secondary
traits. The figure of *Sapience*, wholly alive,
active and adored, is only to be found in the
Cabala, and it is only from there that Spenser
could have taken her so easily, in one of those
periods when, frightened by the mutability of
the things of this world, he looked for help to a
higher world.

Let us analyse, first of all, the characteristics of
*Sapience* as Spenser describes them. To bring
as much objectivity as possible to this analysis, I
will not classify the traits, but will give them in
the same order as in the hymn.

In the first place, the special character of *Sapience's* relations with the Deity is marked from the
first lines:

* See the passage quoted below.
† See Legouis, *Spenser*, p. 43.

There in his bosome Sapience doth sit,
The soveraine dearling of the Deity.

And the poet returns to it further on:

And those most sacred mysteries unfold
Of that fair love of mightie heavens king.

And again:

And (God) lets his own Beloved to behold.

*Sapience* is dressed as a queen, adorned with jewels and pearls, and wears a golden crown.

she holds the sceptre of God, rules over his house, over heaven and over earthly creatures;

all creatures are parts of her, and remain what God made them by obeying her laws; it was through her that Creation came about;

she reflects the face of God himself, and passes all human understanding;

her beauty fills heaven and dims the earth. Mortals can see her;

she overwhelms them with favours; God has given her his heavenly treasures;

no one can share in these treasures except through her; she is the mediator between God and man;

men who see her are full of rapture;

she is the sovereign light.

We will take these traits one by one, and find

them again in the *Schekhina*. The sexual character
may be interpreted at will as an allegory or as a
sublimated expression of the sensuality which is
certainly one of the dominant traits of the character and poetry of Spenser. This is equally true in
the Cabala. The sexual relations between God
and the *Schekhina* are a subject for scandal to the
uninitiated, and are also capable of allegorical
interpretation. But, at all events, they are certainly
the highest expression of the sensuality which fills
the *Zohar* (it is probably this trait which forms
the chief difference between the Schekhina of the
*Zohar* and the Wisdom of the Bible).

We will be content with one or two quotations
from the *Zohar* in proof of this: "The desire of
the One on high is aroused in love for the *Schekhina*, like to the desire of the male for the female"
(i. 66*b*).

In i. 27*b* the French translator is obliged to take
refuge in Latin, so very detailed does the description of the *Schekhina* become.

In i. 60*b* we are told it is to these relations
allusion is made when it is written, "The Holy
One, blessed be his name, walks about and takes
his pleasure with the souls of the righteous"; and
the "mysteries" of the love of God for the *Schekhina* are explained at length. This gives the matter
for Spenser's lines:

And those most sacred mysteries unfold
Of that faire love of mightie heavens King.

As to the ornaments and clothing of the *Schekhina*, the subject is a commonplace one in the *Zohar*, and the details are numerous. On the crown the following passage is perhaps more interesting:

"When the Holy One, blessed be his name, sets on his head the sacred and heavenly crowns, the patriarchs are also crowned. Seeing the patriarchs crowned, the *Matrona* crowns herself and then the blessings of heaven are poured forth everywhere."*

*Sapience* holds the sceptre of God and rules over his house.

*Zohar* ii. 57*a*:

"Then the king said to himself: the whole world must learn of the high qualities of my Matrona . . . all the powers of the king are entrusted to the Matrona . . . all his arms . . . all the captains of his hosts . . . all the gems and royal treasures."

*Sapience* rules over the heavens, over earthly creatures, because it was through her that creation came about:

> For of her fulness which the world does fill
> They all partake, and do in state remaine
> As their great Maker did at first ordaine,
> Through observation of her high beheast
> By which they first were made, and still increast.

* ii. 52a (Vol. III., p. 234).

The *Tiqouné Zohar* xix. tells us:

"At the beginning of Genesis there is none but
Elohim which denotes the Schekhina, because all
which was created, from the Hayoth and the
Seraphim down to the smallest earth worm, live
in Elohim and through Elohim . . . for the creation is the work of the *Schekhina*, and she watches
over it as a mother watches over her children."

In the *Zohar* i. 22a, "Supreme Wisdom on
high," "the mother," says, "I desire to create
man in my image," while God hesitated to create
man (foreseeing sin). This is therefore "her fulness
which the world does fill," and here is:

. . . observation of her high beheast
By which they first were made, and still increast.

"It is written: 'The Lord God has established
the Earth through Wisdom' . . . when the Holy
One, blessed be his name, created the world, *he
saw that it could not exist without the Law;* therefore he created the Law which contains all laws"
(II. 428-429).

And God declares:

"It is through the Schekhina that I cause the
wicked to die, it is through her that I cause the
righteous to live" (I. 140).

Sapience reflects the face of God and passes all
human understanding; it is she who is the sovereign light; the three characteristics go together:

"When the Holy· One, blessed be his name, created the world . . . he engraved the letters. Yod represents the central Point . . . from this mysterious Point issues a slender ray· of Light (which is the *Schekhina*) which, although *also hidden and invisible*, contains all lights. This slender ray of light receives the vibration of Him who does not vibrate, and reflects the light of Him who sheds no light . . ." (These vibrations constitute in some way the embrace of God and the *Schekhina*.)*

Her name is Beauty, the hymn being entitled "Of heavenly Beautie"; in the explanation of "the cloud that is always seen around the *Schekhina*" it is said that

"The sacred names form a triangle; one side of this triangle wears the crown of Mercy, another side wears the crown of Wrath . . . and the third is clothed in purple, the garment of the supreme and holy king called Beauty" (III. 233).

This triple aspect of the *Schekhina*—Mercy, Wrath, Beauty—is in harmony with the character of Sapience, who is Law, who is Beauty and who is revealed by the Mercy of God:

> thrise happy man him hold
> Of all on earth, whom God so much doth grace
> And lets his own Beloved to behold.

* de Pauly's note, IV. 5.

This Beauty fills heaven:

"The vibrations felt by the slender ray form around it luminous waves. . . . It is thus that the slender ray of light gives rise to a world of light caused by the waves" (iv. 5).

The righteous are permitted to see Sapience, and the sight of her is bliss:

> thrise happy man him hold
> Of all on earth . . .

*Zohar* ii. 210*ab*:

"The righteous contemplate this light and are illumined by the rays of the supreme Light. But on each Sabbath the *Schekhina* manifests herself more clearly" (let us recall Spenser's prayer at the end of the fragment "Mutability": "O thou great Sabbaoth God, grant me that Sabbaoth's sight!")*

"All the righteous then come and bow down before her. Happy the lot of him who gains possession of the garments with which the righteous are clothed in Paradise" (IV. 219).

Finally, Sapience is the sole mediator: God has bestowed on her his treasures, and no one shares in them save through her:

> None thereof worthy be but those whom she
> Vouchsafeth to her presence to receave . . .

* Church and Todd suggest "That Sabbath's sight"; a very acceptable correction.

The eternal portion of her precious dowre,
Which mighty God has given to her free,
And to all those which thereof worthy be.

In the *Zohar*, God declares:
"From this day forth none may have speech
with me, without first having speech with the
*Matrona*. Thus the Matrona is the perfect mediator with God, and all power is in her hands, and
this is what makes the glory of the *Matrona*" (Vol.
III., p. 231).

Thus, therefore, from the names "Wisdom" and
"Beauty" to the principal attributes: the character of wife and mistress of the house of the Deity;
the character of creator of Law and reward for the
Righteous; the character of sole mediator; and
even to the secondary and more ordinary attributes:
light, splendour, adornment, etc., all the traits of
*Sapience* are to be found in the *Schekhina*; and no
general objection is evident as in the case of the
previous hypotheses of Plato's Beauty, the Virgin
Mary or the Holy Spirit.

It must be noted, moreover, that the character
of the *Schekhina*, who represents the feminine
part of the Deity (a part necessary to creation,
since the creation is represented as a cosmic act
corresponding to the sexual act), is in harmony
with the poetic presentment of Nature philosophy
in "The Garden of Adonis." There, the union
of Venus and Adonis results in creation. The

hypothesis of the *Schekhina* being the source of
inspiration for *Sapience* enables us to see in
"The Garden of Adonis" the expression of ideas
which are not merely an intellectual pastime on
Spenser's part, but which are in harmony with
his "Christian" philosophy. This establishes a
connection between his two forms of expression
—the pagan and the Christian. This connection
is important: as we have seen, the ideas expressed
by Spenser may be divided into two entirely
separate groups. In *The Faërie Queene* ("Garden
of Adonis" and "Mutability Cantos") Spenser
shows himself to be strongly impressed by the
vicissitudes of human life and of Nature. His
thinking (if carried to its furthest extent—and he
appears to have done so, but to have rather
clumsily disguised the fact, in the "Mutability
Cantos") leads him to scepticism: all things
change, therefore all things are mortal; man's
soul changes, therefore . . . he takes the argument
from Lucretius, but takes care not to come to a
conclusion, probably because he finds the conclusion too startling, even in the mouth of Mutability, although she is to be condemned:

And men themselves do change continually
—Ne do their bodies only flit and fly
But eeke their minds which they immortall
call
Ne is the water in more constant case . . .

234

On the other hand, in the last hymns Spenser shows himself, in the main, as orthodox, and gives utterance to nothing which a cultured puritan of his time could not accept. Spenser takes refuge in a higher world where the vicissitudes of change have no place. This solution, indicated rather hesitatingly in the hurried end of the "Mutability Cantos," is the true orthodox solution, developed at the end of the hymns: Let us renounce this world and seek refuge in the Deity.

But in this deity Spenser hopes to find the characteristics he had loved in Nature in his pagan poems: love, and love in its most engaging form; in God himself he hopes to find sexual life. Thus the cabalistic conception enables us to establish some unity in his intellectual and sentimental life.

Let us now compare the endings of the two religious hymns. The ideas are the same; we must love God, Spenser tells us at the end of Hymne III.:

Then shalt thou feel thy spirit so possest
And ravished with devouring great desire
Of his dear self, that shall thy feeble brest
Inflame with love, and set thee all on fire. . . .

But the poet is addressing the world in general; the personal relationship between him, the poet, and the Deity is not established; the theme goes off into generalisations. At the end of Hymne IV. the same idea is expressed, but the feeling is much stronger; it is through Sapience that this result is obtained:

> None thereof worthy be, but those whom she
> Vouchsafeth to her presence to receave
> And letteth them her lovely face to see
> Whereof such wondrous pleasures they conceave
> And sweet contentment, that it doth bereave,
> Their soul of sense, through infinite delight
> And them transport from flesh into the spright....

The whole end of Hymne III. is transposed into a more ardent mood; but it is especially through Sapience that, in the two last stanzas of Hymne IV., the personal relationship between the poet and God is established; and the series of hymns concludes on this personal note:

> Ah then, my hungry soul! which long hast fed
> On idle fancies of thy foolish thought,
> Ah! cease to gaze on matter of thy grief
> And look at last up to that sovereign light,
> From whose pure beams al perfect beauty springs,
> That kindleth love in every godly spright
> Even the love of God . . .
> Thy straying thoughts henceforth for ever rest.

It is Sapience who leads him to God, who reveals to him the love of God; it is through her that he communes with the divine love. This is a noteworthy fact, since to the orthodox Christian, to the normal puritan, this mediator is the Son, Jesus Christ. The *Wisdom* of the Christian does not play this rôle. To the cabalists, on the contrary, who usually ignore Jesus Christ, the vessel of divine love is the *Schekhina*, Wisdom, Sapience.

So, far more than in the details of the person of Sapience, it is in this identical rôle of Sapience and the *Schekhina*, whereas usually divine love is associated with the rôle of Jesus Christ, that we can see a cabalistic influence on the conceptions and even on the feelings of Spenser.

# CONCLUSION

We have thus found in Spenser a first example of philosophical poetry at the very beginning of modern English literature. The general characteristics of the philosophical poet, as defined in our earlier chapters, are evident in him. It is impossible to establish scientifically his connection with the occult tradition; but if we are not willing to accept it, then our last chapter becomes an even more striking proof of the similarity between his mind and the minds of the rabbis of the *Zohar*. So perfect indeed seems the proof that it is, I think, easier to admit a direct influence, however unproved, than so complete a parallelism in thought and feeling.

In either case, our general thesis stands clear, and, bearing it in mind, we can understand better Milton's enthusiasm—for Milton also knew of the Cabala—when he wrote in the *Areopagitica* of "our sage and serious poet Spenser, whom I dare be known to think a better teacher than Scotus and Aquinas."

A statement that gives cause for thought, not only about Spenser, but about philosophical poetry as a whole.

# APPENDIX

## TRANSLATIONS OF PASSAGES QUOTED FROM FOREIGN AUTHORS

Page 11. *Aus heimischer Tiefe* . . .
> From secret depths,
> From sleep which is thought.

*Mein Schlaf ist Träumen* . . .
> My sleep is dreaming,
> My dreaming is thinking.

*Wo Wesen sind* . . .
> Where beings live,
> There is thy breath.

Page 13. *Dieser alte Heilige* . . .
> This old hermit, in his wood, has not yet heard the news that God is dead.

*In dein Auge* . . .
> Into thine eye have I looked, O Life, and I felt myself sinking into the unfathomable.

Page 15. *Mein Schlaf ist Träumen* . . .
> My sleep is dreaming,
> But when I sleep,
> The Norns are awake;
> They weave the rope,
> They unwind my knowledge piously:
> Why do you not ask the Norns?

*Um sie kein Ort,* . . .
> Round them no Space, still less Time,
> One cannot speak about them.
> The Mothers are they.

Page 19. *Die Mütter! Mütter!* . . .
> The Mothers! Mothers! it sounds so weird!

# APPENDIX

Page 24. . . . *Sans quoi, sur la même* . . .
Otherwise, on the same level,
The created being equal to the creator,
This perfection, lost in the infinite,
Would be reabsorbed in Him,
And creation, become too resplendent,
Would have gone back into God and would not have
existed.

Page 26. *Place à tout,* . . .
Give way to the all! I am Pan! Jupiter! kneel to me.

Page 28. *bekannt ist dir* . . .
Thou knowest
What is hidden in the abyss;
And what pervades
Mountains and valleys, wind and water.
Where beings live
There is thy breath:
Where brains think
There is thy thinking.

Page 29. *Comme sur le versant* . . .
As on the slope of a prodigious mountain,
A vast medley of confused sound, from the dark abyss
Thou canst see the terrifying creation coming towards thee.
The rock is further, the animal nearer.
Thou deemest thyself the highest peak of life—
But tell me, canst thou believe the world deceives us,
And this ladder, that it breaks?
Never, it goes on, unconquerable, wonderful,
Into the invisible, the imponderable,
And there disappears—to thy eyes.

*Vous ferez alliance* . . .
You will make alliance even with the beasts,
For God created them and wants you to love them.
Of instinct, of intelligence in various degrees
They have their share; acknowledge it,
Discover in their eyes, precarious as a dream,
The dawn of reason that begins and grows.
You shall not put out this uncertain light,
A presage of splendour and immortality.
You shall respect it since angels respect it.
The thousand links go from man to the insect,

But the first, the last, the intermediate,
You shall not despise the least of them, for all lead up to God.

Page 30.   *Wolfe, der war* . . .
            The Wolf, he was my father.

            *Zum Jagen zog* . . .
            To the hunting went
            With the youth the man;
            From wood and mountain.
            Once when they came back
            The Wolf's lair was empty:
                For many years
                Lived the youth
            With the Wolf in the wild fores
                They also
                Were much hunted.

Page 31.   *der Jäger viele* . . .
                Many of the hunters
                Fell to the Wolf;
            In flight through the forest
            The Wild One drove them;
            But I was parted from my father:
                I lost his tracks,
                The skin of a Wolf
            Only did I find in the forest.

            *jetzt dem Wurfe* . . .
            And now the offspring of the She-Wolf
            Thou bringest to the feet of thy wife.

Page 33.   *Afrique aux plis infranchissables,* . . .
            Africa with thy impenetrable folds,
            Depth of horizons sinister, sea of sand,
            Sahara, Dahomey, Nagaïn, Darfour . . .
            Landscapes in moonlight where fear prowls,
            The Outang walks erect, holding a club,
            Nature has passed beyond reason and man.

Page 34.   *Oh! si la conjecture* . . .
            Oh! should the ancient guess be then a fact,
            The awful dream of the Chaldean priest,
            The thought of Hermes and Pythagoras,
            Should the old nightmare be the truth indeed  . . .
            Terrible creatures that live in the dark,

The flattened heads of tiger and serpent,
The heads on which the divine heel has pressed,
The bear in gloom, the ape, man of the awful forest,
O heavens! were that to be truth, that those are
They whom we call the damned, in their torment.
> *Toute faute qu'on fait* . . .
The sin committed is a jail opened.
The murderer, when death taps on his shoulder
And awakes him, terrified, recognises the prison
Built by his crime crawling after him.
Tiberius is a rock, Sejanus a snake.

Page 37. *Wer keinen Namen* . . .
> He who has won no name for himself nor has any
> noble ambition
> Belongs to the elements; therefore begone!

Page 40. *Ainsi que le soleil* . . .
> Even as the sun draws upwards the cloud,
> And fills it with the rainbow,
> God by his puissant look draws upwards the dark,
> From the funeral abyss
> Where even evil prayed to him,
> And all things monstrous that stammer his Name.
> And he puts back, among all the worlds of glory,
> This world of shame.

Page 48. *Quel dieu, quel moissonneur* . . .
> What God, harvester of eternal sheaves,
> Had, turning homeward, thrown away at random
> This golden sickle in the starry field.

Page 49. *Les morts, les pauvres morts* . . .
> For surely the poor dead do suffer much,
> And when October that despoils old trees
> Blows his dreary wind all round their tombstones,
> Surely they think the living most ungrateful.

Page 50. *Les morts que l'on fait saigner* . . .
> The dead, whom someone causes still to bleed,
> Claim vengeance always.
> In their own way they take it, and pitiable
> Are those who fall under their silent blows.
> Better never to have known what life is,
> Better a slow death, many times repeated—
> So long the period, so heavy the blows.

# INDEX

## INDEX